DOG TRAINING FOR KIDS

DOG TRAINING FOR KIDS

FUN & EASY WAYS TO TAKE CARE OF YOUR FURRY FRIEND

VANESSA ESTRADA MARIN

FOREWORD BY FROLIC

co-written with L. Ryan Storms
and illustrated by Alisa Harris

Every dog is unique. If you have any questions or concerns,
be sure to consult a veterinarian or a professional dog expert.

ISBN: 9780593196571
Ebook ISBN: 9780593196625

Book design by Aimee Fleck

Printed in the United States of America
7 9 10 8

First Edition

To my canine soul mate, Comet.
Because of you, my heart is always open
to loving and doing more for others.

Table of Contents

④ CLEVER TRICKS 80

⑤ SUPER FUN GAMES 120

Frolic is excited for kids to learn more about dogs! Did you know that humans and dogs developed a close relationship over 10,000 years ago? Not only are dogs integral for our survival, but they also teach us and help us practice responsibility, empathy, and compassion. Because of dogs, we can be better versions of ourselves.

But many of us never get to enjoy the true company of a dog because most kids—and adults!—are not quite ready for that kind of commitment. Training and taking care of a dog takes true work and responsibility. That's why Frolic exists and why we are so excited about this book!

Through Frolic's programming and our director and author of this book, Vanessa, we have helped people connect with man's and woman's best friend. One of our favorite successes to date is Ron and Tessa— grade schoolers whose parents reached out to us when the kids really wanted to get a dog. The parents, remembering that their parents got stuck taking care of their dogs, were hesitant to oblige. Completing many of the same exercises and tutorials in this book as well as two long-weekend sleepovers with Frolic dogs, Ron and Tessa graduated from our Canine Companion program and proved that they were great dog trainers and caretakers. As a result, they welcomed and currently enjoy the company of a four-month-old Basenji named Xena!

By picking up this book, you are taking your first steps toward understanding what a dog's unconditional love can teach us. Because of your special bond with your canine friend, you will learn skills and lessons that you will use and carry with you as you grow to be the best version of yourself!

DAVID MAHER
Head of Client Happiness
Frolic
NYC

Introduction

Congratulations on deciding to bring a new dog into your family! Your new friend will be so lucky to have you. You're taking on the special responsibility of giving your canine companion an amazing life. By reading this book, you are already showing the love and dedication that you have for your furry bestie.

Your loyal buddy is counting on you to teach them how to manage in your world. Whether you are adopting an adult dog or getting a young puppy, every lesson in this book can be used with any age or breed. All these lessons are designed to be easy for kids and turn every learning experience into a bonding experience for you and your pooch!

Because you will both be new friends to each other, it's important to practice safety while training your dog. Be sure to have an adult there to supervise you and your dog, especially as you get started with training.

1

YOU'RE GETTING A DOG!

You are about to embark on a friendship full of wet kisses, tail wags, belly rubs, and lots of adventures. Welcoming a dog into your life is one of the most exciting things you can experience. How long have you been waiting and begging for this? The funny thing is, once you have your long-awaited dog, taking care of them can seem like a lot of work at first. They eat and drink, they pee and poop, they need exercise, and of course, they need love. It can feel like a lot—dogs need so much attention! But once things calm down and you start to understand each other, you'll create a routine that works for you and your dog.

So before you bring your pup home, let's go over some things you'll want to know, and some helpful ways to make your dog's introduction to their new family and home a safe and happy experience for everyone.

What to Expect from Your Dog

Did you know you can speak to your dog—and your dog can learn to understand you? Training your dog is all about learning how to communicate with each other. But before you can give your dog any commands, you'll need to understand how dogs "speak" to us. At the same time, your dog will be learning to trust you. Your home is a new world; it's full of strange smells, sounds, people, and maybe even other animals, if you have other pets, your dog will be curious about all of it, and you'll be their guide. So let's talk about how to get to know each other better and build a great friendship full of love, trust, and understanding.

 ## DOG BEHAVIORS & WHAT THEY MEAN

Learning and respecting your dog's behaviors will help them trust you even more. And this will make you a better trainer for your dog! Here are some important dog behaviors and their meanings:

SHAKING OFF. If you've ever given a dog a bath or come in from the rain together, you've probably been in the splash zone and gotten soaked as the dog shakes the water off their back. Sometimes, after a dog gets a hug or has an energetic play session, they may also shake their fur. This is the dog version of "walking off" a feeling or emotion. This helps the dog reset how they are feeling and continue with their day feeling calmer.

SNIFFING BUTTS. To humans, it's a little gross—to dogs, it's important information! Dogs use their nose to gather information about everyone and everything around them. A dog's sense of smell is very powerful—at least 10,000 times more sensitive than ours! So, by sniffing legs, shoes, or even butts, dogs can "smell" if a person or dog is friendly, sick, or someone they have met before.

ZOOMIES. Have you ever seen a dog running around in a way that looks like they might never stop? This is called "zoomies," or bursts of energetic playtime. This can mean that a dog is overstimulated or that they didn't get enough exercise during the day. They need to burn extra energy before resting, so they bring on the zoomies.

DIGGING. Dogs dig to escape, create a hiding area, track animals, or make a cool spot to lie on, especially during warm weather. Have you ever seen a dog "dig" inside, like into a blanket or bed? This helps them create a comfortable spot to lie on. This behavior happens most often at night and during nap times, and it's completely normal.

POOP SNACKING. *No, Buddy, don't eat that!* While this behavior is icky, it is very common, especially with puppies. Puppies may do this to keep their area clean. Older dogs may also do this for many reasons, such as to avoid getting in trouble for having an accident in the home, to get attention, to stave off boredom, or even to get missing nutrients. The best way to respond is to quickly and calmly clean up after your dog and not be alarmed or make a big deal of it if you find your dog eating their poop. Try to distract them with a dog toy so you can remove the poop from the scene.

PLAY BITING. If a dog gently bites you while playing, they are "mouthing." The way that we play with dogs is different from the way dogs play with their other dog friends. When dogs play with each other, they body-check, mount (climb on top of), or even play bite each other, all of which is normal for dogs. It's important to teach a dog as early as possible what are acceptable forms of play with humans and with dogs. We will talk about how to introduce dogs to other dogs and make sure they're having fun while playing. You'll also learn to show dogs how to use polite behavior with humans.

TAIL CHASING. A dog chasing their tail can be so funny to watch. If a puppy does this, they are probably exploring their body. Dogs can also chase their tail as a way of getting attention.

Finding a Dog That's Right for You

If you're still deciding on what dog to get or if you're wondering how your dog's personality matches with yours and your family's, this section will be helpful. First, consider your own personality and your family's lifestyle. Some things to think about:

AGE. Puppies need a LOT of your time. Young puppies should not be alone for longer than two to three hours at a time. They need us to be around to help them with potty training and socialization. A puppy that is left alone for too long can begin to show destructive behavior or separation anxiety. If you don't have lots of time for a puppy, consider an older puppy or adult dog. They may already be housebroken, comfortable in a crate, and not feel too anxious when left alone at home.

ADOPTION. Dogs are in shelters for many reasons. Some pet parents cannot afford to keep caring for their dog. Some dogs may have gotten lost, and because they don't have any identification, they couldn't be reunited with their family. You can find a lot of mixed-breed dogs in shelters—this can be a lot of fun because they have the qualities and personalities of several different breeds!

ENERGY LEVEL. Energetic breeds such as terriers and retrievers need more exercise than just potty walks. If you're looking for more of a couch potato pup, there are lots of options, such as greyhounds or Cavalier King Charles spaniels. If you really want a high-energy dog but your family has a more relaxed lifestyle, consider dogs from the desired breed that are four years and older.

HAIR OR FUR. People with allergies can still have a dog. Some breeds have hair coats, not fur coats. These dogs tend to shed less, and their coats hold less dust and dander, which cause many animal-related allergies. Some breeds with hair coats include poodles, Italian greyhounds, shih tzus, and Yorkshire terriers.

GROOMING NEEDS. "Fancy" breeds like Maltese and poodles need haircuts and brush-outs to prevent matting (tangles) and reduce shedding. This means they need a trip to the groomer at least once a month, plus regular grooming at home. Are you and your family ready for that? If so, you'll need to have the right tools for your dog's coat to keep their skin and hair healthy.

DOGS, DOGS, DOGS!

BREED GROUP	WHAT THEY ARE KNOWN FOR	HOW THEY ACT & BEHAVE	SIZE & WEIGHT	TYPES OF DOGS
HERDING	Has instincts to gather other animals. Often trained to help farmers group or move herds of animals.	• Intelligent and eager to learn, these dogs do well if they are kept busy. • Can get bored without a routine or "work" to do. • An active family is the best match.	20 lb to 70 lb	Cardigan and Pembroke Welsh corgi, Australian shepherd, Australian cattle dog, German shepherd, border collie
SPORTING	Originally bred to hunt birds or small game.	• Alert, active, and easy to train. • They make great family dogs. • Larger sporting dogs sometimes work as service dogs. • Does best when they are being mentally and physically exercised. They love regular routines.	35 lb to 80 lb	Nova Scotia duck tolling retriever, Labrador retriever, golden retriever, cocker spaniel, flat coated retriever, pointer, vizsla, Irish setter
WORKING	Bred to do jobs like guarding property or livestock or pulling sleds.	• Not recommended for first-time pet owners. • Intelligent and stubborn, so they can be difficult to train. • Because of their physical power, size, and stubbornness, working dogs do best with early training by an experienced trainer. • Incredibly loyal to their families and will keep them out of harm's way.	55 lb to over 200 lb	Giant schnauzer, boxer, Bernese mountain dog, bullmastiff, cane corso, Doberman pinscher, Great Dane, Portuguese water dog, Akita, Alaskan malamute

BREED GROUP	WHAT THEY ARE KNOWN FOR	HOW THEY ACT & BEHAVE	SIZE & WEIGHT	TYPES OF DOGS
HOUNDS	Bred to be hunting dogs.	• Very strong sense of smell. • Except for bloodhounds and basset hounds, they have excellent stamina and are very fast. • Be careful around other small animals, since hounds want to chase and track them. • Training them to have leash manners will be made much easier with a **head halter** or **gentle leader** walking tool (see page 14).	As small as dachshunds at 11 lb or as large as Irish wolfhounds at 140 lb	Basenji, beagle, dachshund, bloodhound, basset hound, greyhound, Irish wolf-hound, whippet, Rhodesian ridgeback
TERRIERS	Bred to "go to the ground," or chase and catch vermin, rodents, and even foxes.	• Very energetic dogs. • Clever and intelligent. • Does best with an active family who can physically tire the dog out. • When bored, the mischievous terrier will find good (and bad) ways to entertain themselves. • If socialized early and properly, terriers can do well with other dogs and children.	Yorkshire terriers can be as small as 4 lb. The largest is the Airedale terrier, weighing as much as 65 lbs.	Yorkshire terrier, cairn terrier, rat terrier, Jack Russell terrier, Airedale terrier, bull terrier, Manchester terrier, Scottish terrier, miniature schnauzer, Staffordshire terrier, Boston terrier
TOY	Bred primarily to be companion dogs	• Great for first-time owners and apartments. • Toy dogs can be very protective of themselves. These dogs yip or nip when they are simply defending themselves. • Smart and loves attention. Great at learning tricks and obedience training.	6 lb (Chihuahuas) to 20 lb (pugs).	Chihuahua, Cavalier King Charles spaniel, Chinese crested, Italian greyhound, Havanese, Maltese, Japanese Chin, miniature pinscher, Pomeranian, pug, shih tzu, toy poodle

Preparing for Your Dog's Arrival

Preparing your home for your new dog is so exciting! You'll want to know what behaviors to expect. For example, puppies are curious because of their age, so you will need to plan ahead to make sure their new home is safe for them. But it's not just puppies—any dog will want to explore their new environment. You can set yourself and your dog up for success by working with your family to inspect each room before your new friend arrives. Here we'll explore how.

 DOG-PROOFING

A dog's nature is to smell, taste, chew, paw, and bark at unfamiliar things. Get down on your knees and look around, yep, just like a dog! By seeing the world through a dog's eyes, you can guess which things might be interesting and make changes that will protect your dog when they are exploring.

These suggestions are just for starters. Once you get to know your dog's personality, you may be able to relax the "rules" a little bit. For example, once you see that your dog has no interest in the bathroom, you can probably keep the bathroom door open—but you may still want to close the toilet lid to make sure they don't think it's their personal drinking bowl!

KITCHEN

Dogs love kitchens, and why not? The kitchen area is full of smells and flavors that can be tempting for any dog, no matter their age. You can keep your dog out of the kitchen when someone is cooking or eating by using a baby gate as a barrier. You can also crate your dog with a delicious chew toy or treat so they don't feel like they're missing out. This will also help once you teach your dog commands such as "Place" (page 69), "Stay" (page 74), and "Leave it" (page 77).

To keep your pup away from chemicals and human snacks, you can work with a grown-up to dog-proof low cabinets with child safety locks. Since dogs love to chew, you'll want to move wires, cords, and cables out of reach, or cover them with cord protectors. Trash bins should have tight-fitting lids. Even the smallest dogs will knock over trash bins. Not only will that make a big mess, but also the dog may snack on food that can make them sick.

FOODS THAT ARE BAD FOR DOGS

Dogs will eat every single food put in front of them. But not all foods are good for dogs. Keep them safe by knowing what foods can be harmful or deadly, and keeping these foods tightly sealed and out of your dog's reach at all times. If your dog gets hold of these, tell an adult so they can get them medical help.

GRAPES AND RAISINS. Grapes and raisins are very dangerous and can lead to kidney failure in dogs. If you drop one, pick it up right away. Also, beware of foods containing these ingredients, such as oatmeal raisin cookies or even grape juice.

CHOCOLATE. Chocolate is unsafe for dogs. It is even unsafe for cats, too. Chocolate contains chemicals theobromine and caffeine, which can cause serious illness. If you want to make a dog-safe "chocolatey" treat for your dog, look for dog treat recipes that use carob chips as an alternative (see recipe websites on page 158).

ALLIUMS. What's an allium? Well, onions, garlic, chives, and leeks are all from the allium species of plants. These ingredients are found in so many dishes, sauces, gravies, and even lower-quality dog foods and treats! Avoid feeding a dog anything with onions or garlic, or even onion powder or garlic powder. Allium toxicosis can cause anemia, which will affect your dog's health.

XYLITOL. Xylitol is found in gum, mouthwash, toothpaste, foods labeled as sugar-free, medications, and deodorants. It is safe for humans, but for dogs, it can cause liver failure or a comatose state.

AVOCADO. No chips and guac for dogs! The high fat content in avocado can cause inflammation of the pancreas, and that big avocado pit can be a choking hazard.

NUTS. Some nuts are harmful to dogs for different reasons. Almonds are not toxic but can cause an upset stomach. Walnuts and pecans can cause seizures. Macadamia nuts can cause pancreatitis and neurological issues. Peanuts and natural peanut butters are safe, but too much can lead to an upset stomach.

COOKED BONES. Cooked bones are dangerous for dogs because the bone is brittle, which means that it can splinter easily. Broken pieces can harm your dog's mouth or even their organs if swallowed. Be especially careful not to give your dog pork or rib bones, even when raw. These types of bones are most likely to splinter.

APPLE SEEDS. This one is tricky. A dog can enjoy a crisp apple slice as a treat but they should never eat apple seeds, which can make them sick.

COFFEE. Coffee has caffeine, which makes your heart beat faster. For a dog, a faster heart rate can be dangerous.

LIVING ROOM

Think like a dog. What would you like to chew on or rub against? Living rooms have all kinds of interesting items, such as power cords, televisions, bookshelves, planters, cushions, lamps, and pillows. To make your living room safe, talk to your grown-up about some of the following fixes:

▷ Mount heavy furniture like TVs and bookshelves to a wall so they don't get knocked over.

▷ Move cords out of reach or cover them so dogs don't chew on them and get an electric shock.

▷ Keep planters (especially those with toxic or dangerous plants) out of reach.

▷ Provide other toys for your dog to chew on, or they might turn to plush items like cushions and pillows!

BEDROOM

This room can be a treasure chest for canine mischief. A dog chewing on a shoe is a very common sight! Look around and be sure to:

▷ Store any items you want to keep out of your pup's mouth in bins, closed closets, and drawers.

▷ Use a tall, covered hamper to prevent your dog from nibbling on your dirty clothes.

▷ Keep smaller items such as jewelry, pencils, and loose change out of reach.

▷ Inspect your room daily. This is an important step if you have a puppy or a dog who chews. Your pet doesn't know that you don't want your favorite shirt chewed up!

BATHROOM

Dogs can find trouble anywhere, even in a bathroom. Talk with your family about these safety ideas:

▷ Until you get to know your dog's habits, keep the bathroom door closed when not in use. They might eat toilet paper, pieces of bathmat, or towels, which can create a blockage in your dog's intestine.

▷ Keep toothpastes, mouthwash, and deodorants out of reach. They can be extremely toxic to dogs.

▷ Keep bathroom cabinets and trash bins tightly closed.

▷ Close the toilet bowl or ask an adult to install a childproof latch on the toilet bowl.

GARAGE/BASEMENT

▷ Ask your grown-ups to store all chemicals such as fertilizer, cleaners, paint, anti-freeze, oil, gas, and lighter fluid out of your dog's reach.

▷ If you have a water heater, boiler, or furnace in your garage or basement, use a dog playpen to create a barrier. This will prevent your dog from burning themselves if they get too close to this hot appliance.

BACKYARD

If you have a yard, you will likely spend a lot of time playing with your dog there. This can be one of the best parts of owning a dog—as long as they don't run away! Dogs can run away for many reasons: they may get startled, or decide to chase an animal or car. This can be dangerous, since a dog doesn't know to look both ways before crossing the road! You can prevent escape by fencing in your outdoor area, either with a regular fence or invisible fencing.

▷ If you can't have a fence, keep a long leash on your dog while outside. This way they'll be able to run around without going too far, so you have a better chance of stopping them from going too far out of sight.

▷ If you already have a fence around your property, check to make sure there are no gaps big enough for your dog or another animal to fit through.

▷ Try never to leave your dog outside unsupervised, because dogs can get themselves into trouble, such as eating things they shouldn't eat or getting tangled in their lead.

CITY DOGS

Being a dog owner in a busy city can be fun, but it's also challenging. Cities are full of sights, sounds, and smells that can be overwhelming for a dog if they feel unsafe. Here are some tips:

USE A LEASH SIX FEET IN LENGTH OR SHORTER. This will help you control your dog in shared spaces such as elevators, staircases, and narrow walkways. Retractable leashes (the kind that spring back automatically) are not good for high-traffic areas because they are not easily seen, they can tangle others, and they allow your dog to be too far away from you.

PAY CLOSE ATTENTION TO WHERE AND WHAT YOUR DOG IS SNIFFING. That pile of garbage may smell great to your dog, but it might be full of unsanitary and dangerous foods. Garbage piles are also where rodents and pests go for snacks. These pests can carry diseases and make you and your dog sick.

GET GOOD WALKING TOOLS FOR YOUR DOG. If your dog constantly has their nose to the ground, pulls, or is always looking for a street snack, there are special walking tools you can buy to train them and make walking them easier (see resources, page 158), such as a gentle leader, head halter, martingale collar or easy walk harness. Leash manners are important when sharing city space!

GIVE YOUR DOG A NAMETAG WITH YOUR FAMILY'S CONTACT INFORMATION. This nametag should have their name and your phone number, at the minimum. Your dog should also wear a current rabies tag on their collar. If they are microchipped, they should have a microchip tag. Many cities require families to register their dog with the local health department. Check with your city or town for the rules.

KEEP YOUR DOG VERY CLOSE TO YOUR SIDE WHEN CROSSING THE STREET. Your dog is shorter than you, so drivers may not see them. Please be careful and stay close.

KNOW THE RULES FOR PUBLIC TRANSPORTATION. This is important for traveling around the city with your dog. Most forms of public transportation allow small dogs on board as long as they fit in an appropriate enclosed pet carrier. Some ride-share services or taxis will permit dogs into their vehicles, as long as they are seated on the floor.

▷ If you have an above- or in-ground pool, it should have its perimeter secured so no dogs (or kids) can get in, plus a covering when not in use.

▷ If your dog will be outside, it is extra important to make sure they have all of their vaccinations and boosters up-to-date.

▷ There are many common plants and fungi that can grow in your yard that your dog may try to eat, some of which can be toxic. This is a good reason to stay with your dog while they're outside.

▷ Ask your grown-ups to avoid putting insecticide or pesticide on your grass, as your dog may eat it and become very ill.

THINGS YOU'LL NEED

There are so many products you can buy for your dog—how do you choose? We'll explore what you will need to buy to give your dog a great quality of life. Once you have the "must-haves," we'll talk about some other nice purchases that can make training and traveling more fun and easy.

😎 MUST-HAVE

COLLAR. Your dog needs a way to wear their ID, rabies tag, and if necessary, their microchip tag and local registration tag. A collar holds all these things and gives you something to hook the leash onto.

LEASH. If you will just use it for leash training and walks, a leash six feet or shorter will do the job. For hiking or exploring in an open area, a retractable leash is another choice that gives dogs a little more freedom to explore.

APPROPRIATE WALKING TOOLS. Does your dog pull or try to run ahead? Once you figure out where your dog needs support in developing proper leash manners, use their walking tools every time you go outside for a walk. This is to ensure your safety, your dog's safety, and the safety of others. See the glossary (page 157) and resources (page 158) for more information on walking tools such as harnesses and special collars.

FOOD. Of course this is a must-have—the question is, what kind? It's a good idea to make this decision with your veterinarian. The right choice for your dog will depend on their age, breed, and nutritional needs. For example, puppy formula is designed

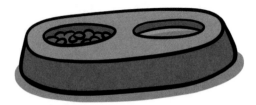

for puppies, and adult dog formulas are created for adult dogs ages 12 months and up. Your vet can tell you about the benefits of dry and canned foods. One more tip: Avoid suddenly changing your dog's diet. Instead, make changes slowly, over the course of 10 days.

LOW-CALORIE TRAINING TREATS. We all love treats, and so do dogs! In this book, we will use different treats (see Low- and High-Value Treats, page 22) to reward good dog behavior. When you teach your dog a task, or help them learn to adjust to an uncomfortable experience, these training treats will help your dog focus.

BOWLS FOR FOOD AND WATER. Your dog should have food served in their dish at mealtimes and have clean water available to them all day. Make sure you clean their bowls every day.

CONFINEMENT SPACE. This may be a crate or a gated area, like a laundry room. This is their safe space, where they can go and relax when they need some "me" time. This space also helps with potty training (page 42). Finally, this space also helps you keep your dog safe when people come to your home to do repair work, or when your family has parties.

CAR TRAVEL SAFETY RESTRAINT. Just as you would wear a seat belt in a car, your dog should also have a safety restraint like a dog seat belt, or dog car seat/carrier. If your dog is unrestrained in the car when there is an accident or if the car makes a sudden stop, they could become injured, and possibly injure other passengers as well. They could also become frightened and want to run away from the situation.

FIRST AID AND EMERGENCY KIT. You can make your own kit, or buy one designed for dogs. This kit may include:

▷ Gauze, dog bandages, and tape

▷ Hydrogen peroxide, milk of magnesia, and/or activated charcoal (for use in case of poisoning)

▷ Antibiotic spray

▷ Extra food and treats

▷ Syringe for flushing wounds or feeding medications

▷ Extra leash, collar, and/or muzzle

This kit should also include their medical records and a dog first aid booklet. Make sure you or a grown-up know how to use the different items before an emergency happens.

FLEA, TICK, AND HEARTWORM PREVENTION. No matter where you live or what the season is, fleas, ticks, and mosquitoes can "bug" your dog and affect their health. You can buy flea, tick, and heartworm chewables from your vet and give them to your dog on the schedule set by the doctor.

POTTY PADS OR NEWSPAPER (FOR POTTY TRAINING PUPS). If your puppy is younger than four months, they may not have all of their vaccinations. To keep them safe from diseases that can be transmitted from other animals, it is best for your pooch to use the potty indoors on potty pads or newspapers.

POOP SCOOP OR POOP BAGS. Nobody likes stepping in poop—not even your dog! Keep spaces clean and always clean up after your dog when they go number two. Plus, your dog's poop can attract bugs such as flies, which will carry bacteria from your dog's feces.

DOG BED OR BLANKET. Dogs like being cozy, too! Provide your dog with something soft and comfortable to call their own when they are relaxing.

GROOMING SUPPLIES. Your dog will need:

▷ A brush

▷ Gentle, dog-safe shampoo and conditioner

▷ A nail clipper

▷ A dog-safe toothbrush

When you brush your dog, you maintain their healthy skin and coat. Dogs with longer fur may need regular grooming. If your dog has a shorter coat, you can bathe them at home. You can also prevent your dog's nails from getting

too long by clipping just the very tips of the nails. Ask the vet or a grown-up for help or to show you how, so you don't cut too much and make their nails bleed. Many dogs don't get proper dental care, but keeping their teeth clean with a dog-safe toothpaste, a foam, or a water additive can help keep their mouth healthy.

ENZYMATIC CLEANER. Dogs and puppies will have accidents in the home, especially while they are still adjusting to their new environment. Let your parents know that an enzymatic cleaner will thoroughly clean urine, feces, vomit, and saliva.

TOYS. Dogs need entertainment, too. If you provide your dog with a variety of appropriate toys, they will stay entertained and hopefully out of trouble, even when you're not home. If you can, offer different toys for each day of the week—this will keep your dog's mind active.

☺ NICE TO HAVE

TREAT POUCH. Having a treat pouch with a belt can make training more fun for you. It also keeps your treats in a safe, easy-to-reach spot, while keeping your hands free to handle your dog.

FOOD MAT. Your dog may make a mess when drinking water or eating their food. Just make sure you clean the germs and old food off of the mat regularly.

EXTRA COLLARS AND LEASHES. As long as it fits, a good-quality collar (and leash) can last a very long time if well cared for and washed regularly. But it can help to have a spare set.

DOG WIPES. These protect your furniture and remove some of the dirt your dog tracks in from the outside world, but you can also just wipe their paws with a damp rag.

DOGGY CAMERA. There are several services that allow you to watch your dog from a computer or a smartphone while you are not home with them. Being able to see them safe (and not getting into mischief) can give you peace of mind, especially when your dog is still adjusting to their new home.

☹ PASS

POOR-QUALITY TOYS. All dog toys aren't the same. Be sure to get durable and comfortable toys for your dog to play with. Once they break a toy, sneak it away from them so they don't eat pieces of rubber, plastic, or cotton stuffing.

DOG STROLLERS. This can be a convenient way to transport an older dog, or a dog that has trouble getting around. Otherwise, it's not necessary.

DOG CLOTHING. Unless your dog has very little or no hair and needs additional warmth or protection from the sun, dogs don't need clothing or costumes.

LUXURY PET BEDS. Puppies especially do not need fancy pet beds. They are still learning to control their bowels and not chew on everything. It is very likely that a puppy will have an accident or chew on it while they are teething, so start with an inexpensive bed with a washable cover. Even a towel or blanket will do for starters.

THE FIRST DAY

The first moments you bring your dog into your new home are so exciting—you'll remember them forever! But this time is also very important to start your dog with a smooth transition into their new adventure. This is a big deal for your dog—they are joining a strange new place with people, sights, and smells that they don't know. These four steps can help you smooth the path for them:

STEP 1: GET YOUR HOME READY. Before bringing your dog home, close off rooms that you don't want your dog entering, and have your dog's crate or gated area already set up. You can provide an old T-shirt or towel with your scent on it so they get familiar with your smell as a comfort. It can help to have a crate cover over the crate to give your dog some privacy in their first few days in your home.

STEP 2: INTRODUCE YOUR HOME USING A LEASH. Walk your dog into your home while they are on a leash. As excited as you are, make sure that your home is calm and quiet, so your dog or puppy doesn't get overwhelmed. While they're on the leash, walk them slowly through the areas of the home where they will be

allowed to roam. You can lead your dog to their confinement space so they can settle in on their own.

STEP 3: SHOW YOUR DOG AROUND THE NEIGHBORHOOD. After some hours or the next day, take your dog on a short walk near your home so they get to know more of their new environment. Make sure their collar fits well and that they seem happy and not stressed or skittish.

STEP 4: WAIT TO INTRODUCE GUESTS. I know you want to show the world your new pup, but try not to invite people or other dogs over to your home to visit for the first few days your dog is home. Instead, let your pup get used to their new home and build a bond with your family members before introducing more new people.

If you have another dog at home, it's a good idea to switch Steps 2 and 3. Have a family member bring your existing dog outside to meet you with your new dog. Try to meet in a neutral spot off your property. You and your family member can take the two dogs on a walk together in your neighborhood before walking the dogs into the home at the same time. Keep both dogs on leashes in the home for the first week while they are still learning about each other—it may seem strange, but your existing dog is also getting used to this big change in their environment!

 # LOW- AND HIGH-VALUE TREATS

Do you like rewards? I think we all do! Rewards help us work harder, get excited about things, and celebrate a job well done. Dogs feel the same way. When you teach your dog the commands and tricks in this book, you'll want to get them excited about learning. We will use both low-value treats and high-value treats, depending on the difficulty of the challenge. So many foods can be used as training snacks. See page 158 for links to articles that will teach you what foods dogs can (and cannot) enjoy.

LOW-VALUE TREATS are usually low-calorie treats such as the dog's dry food, also called kibble. For dogs that eat wet food, low-value treats might be bits of dog biscuit. Small pieces of carrot or apple (without the seeds) are other good snacks.

HIGH-VALUE TREATS are special treats given to encourage a dog to do a more challenging trick. Such treats might include a small nibble of cooked chicken, beef, liver, tuna, deli meat, cheese, or even a small amount of peanut butter.

HOW A VET CAN HELP

Veterinarians have a special understanding and love of animals. Your vet will help you when you need to make decisions about your dog's health and well-being.

FINDING A VET. If you have friends or family members who have dogs, ask them for recommendations! One thing all great veterinarians will have in common is that they are always kind to the animal while being supportive of their human. Try to choose a vet before you bring your dog home.

PREPARING FOR THE VISIT. When you take your dog to the vet for the first time, bring all of your dog's documents with you. You'll need all records of their vaccinations, microchip number, deworming schedule, their date of birth, the date you purchased or adopted them, and information on where they came from. Your vet may ask you to bring a stool (poop) sample to test for parasites.

RIDING WITH YOUR DOG IN THE CAR. It's best to ride with your dog in the backseat. Make sure your dog is secured in their safety restraint. Bring cloth and paper towels, cleaning solution, and a trash bag in case your dog becomes nervous on the ride to and from the vet. They may drool a lot or get carsick.

WAITING IT OUT (IN THE WAITING ROOM). Keep your dog on a leash or in a carrier while you're in the waiting room of the vet's office. Bring some high-value treats (see page 20) to help make this experience a positive one full of rewards for your dog. Don't be surprised, though; if your dog is very stressed, they may refuse to eat. This is normal.

WHAT TO EXPECT. Your vet will begin by weighing your dog on a scale. A smaller dog or puppy will be weighed on a tabletop scale. For a larger dog, there will likely be a scale on the ground. The vet will examine your dog's body, ears, eyes, teeth, and gums. On the first visit, the vet may draw blood to check their health and immune system. Your vet will use the vaccination history you share to determine if your pup needs any vaccinations. If your pup is not yet spayed or neutered, your vet will ask you to consider it. Spaying or neutering your dog is a common procedure that many people find keeps their dogs healthy and better behaved, and reduces their chances of developing certain cancers.

FOLLOWING UP. With the help of an adult, follow up with your vet to ask about any results from stool samples and bloodwork. If everything looks normal and healthy, and you agreed to spay or neuter your dog, you can set up the appointment for that to be done. You can also set up appointments for your dog's next vaccination booster, dental appointment, and checkup.

② BASIC TRAINING LESSONS

It's easier and more fun to have a well-behaved dog than a dog who doesn't know the rules. As your dog's owner, you are also their teacher! You have the power to teach them manners and obedience, and this chapter will show you how. The following basic training tricks are fundamental behaviors—this means you can build on them. Most are tricks your dog can learn right away, so let's get started!

RECOGNIZING THEIR NAME

Teaching a dog their name is important. It teaches them to pay attention to you and to respond to your command. A bonus of teaching a dog their name (and the nicknames you will probably give them) is that it strengthens your bond with each other.

WHAT YOU'LL NEED

▷ **A quiet, small indoor space without distractions**

▷ **A four- to six-foot leash**

▷ **A small bag or pouch of kibble/dry food**

Note: If your dog eats wet food, use small pieces of low-value and low-calorie training treats (see page 20). You can store them in a Ziploc bag while practicing this technique.

STEP 1

Start in a small space, standing close to your dog. Attach the leash and then loosely hold the leash in one hand—you will be using it later. Have a piece of kibble/treat in your other hand, in a fist behind your back. Look away from your dog, and do not make eye contact with them just yet.

STEP 2

After a couple of seconds, look at your dog and say their name once in a happy and excited voice. If they do not turn in your direction or look up at you, wait 10 seconds before trying again. Don't repeat their name over and over again without a break.

STEP 3

As soon as your dog makes eye contact, let them know that they did the right thing by using a happy marker word—this is a short word, like "Nice!" or "Yes!" and give them their treat. This will help them learn that when their name is called, they should look and make eye contact with you or the person who calls their name.

STEP 4

Once your dog can do this while you are loosely holding their leash 10 times in a row (with a 10-second break between each try), you can practice it from a distance by letting go of the leash completely but still being in the same room. Work on this exercise for up to 10 minutes a day, in different rooms in your house, as well as outside.

TIPS

PROBLEM SOLVING

- If your dog is extra clever, they will realize that treats are coming from your other hand. Your dog may start looking for that treat hand and not make eye contact with you when you say their name. Make sure to give them that 10-second break in between each try. Don't pull on their leash to get their attention. Instead, help them by starting over in a different part of the room, giving them a fresh start.

- Be calm, patient, and loving with your dog while teaching them their name, so they learn that their name being called is a good thing!

SAFETY

When giving your dog the treat, try using the hand bowl technique (page 28) to avoid potentially getting nipped!

SIGNALING FOR POTTY

Once your dog is actually potty trained, it doesn't take much to train them to let you know when they need to go out. Some dogs scratch the door with a paw, but to avoid damaging your door, train your pup to use a string of bells!

WHAT YOU'LL NEED

▷ A string of bells (or one bell on a string)

Learn this first: Being Housebroken (page 42)

STEP 1

Tie a string of bells or a single bell on a sturdy string to the doorknob of the door your dog uses to go outside most of the time.

STEP 2

Each time you take your dog out for their bathroom walk, bump the bells with your hand before you open the door. Make sure your dog sees and hears this action. Praise your dog with a marker word after the bells jingle. (Yes, even though you were the one to jingle them. If you want, you can praise yourself, too!)

STEP 3

Praise your dog when they have done their business. Over time, if you always ring the bell, your dog will learn to connect the bells with bathroom and will begin to nose the bells when they feel the urge to go out.

SAFETY

If you let your dog out to go to the bathroom, only let them into a fenced, safe area. Never let your dog off a leash in the open, as they can run into trouble, such as other animals, humans, or cars.

TIPS

PROBLEM SOLVING

- Don't use treats for this training exercise, or your dog may think that ringing the bells means food. (And then they'll always ring the bells at the door, not just when they have to go out.)

TAKING TREATS GENTLY

Dogs are SO excited to get a treat that they may unintentionally hurt us with their teeth as they grab the treat out of our hand. This lesson will teach your dog patience and self-control, as they learn not to grab, but instead to receive treats nicely. The more excitable your dog is, the more patience you'll need while teaching them.

WHAT YOU'LL NEED

▷ **A bag or pouch of your dog's kibble/dry food to use as low-value treats**

Note: If your dog eats wet food, use small pieces of low-value and low-calorie training treats (see page 20).

STEP 1

Begin in a quiet space without distractions (people, toys, loud sounds like the television, other dogs). Have an adult stay with you for this first lesson.

STEP 2

Keep the treats out of sight and out of your dog's reach. Take one treat and close your hand around it into a fist.

STEP 3

Ask your dog to come over by calling their name if they know it. You can also get your pup's attention by patting your lap, clapping your hands, or gently patting the floor and calling them over using a happy, excited voice. (Over time, you'll get to know what gets the best response!)

STEP 4

Show your dog your fist, and gently bring it near their nose. Encourage them to sniff your fist so they know there is a treat waiting for them. ▶

STEP 5

With your fingers facing up, open your fist into the shape of a bowl. Be sure that all of your fingers are closed tightly together. Then, move your "hand bowl" to your dog's nose so they do not have to try and reach the treat with their teeth. Because your hand is so close to their mouth, they will have no choice but to lick the kibble out of your hand.

TIPS

PROBLEM SOLVING

- If your pup paws or tries to nibble at your closed fist, quickly put your fist behind your back and in a high-pitched voice, say, "Uh-oh!" Try again until your dog only sniffs your fist and seems calm.

- Practice the hand bowl technique *before* working with your dog. If your fingers are open or if you open your hand too wide, the treat can fall through your fingers or roll out of your hand, and your dog might try to snap up the treat as it's moving. But if you cup your hand too tightly, your dog won't be able to lick the treat out and may become confused.

PUPPY

Puppies teethe, and so they are looking to chew on anything that may comfort their gums—even their sharp teeth on your hands! Help your puppy understand that your hands are *not* toys to chew on. You can either offer a rubber toy that does not squeak or make a noise as you take your fist away. Don't do both, though, since the combination of hearing "Uh-oh" and then receiving a toy may be confusing for a puppy. 🐾

NOT PULLING ON A LEASH

Dogs don't know that pulling on a leash can be dangerous to them and their human. If you teach your dog polite leash manners, this will allow them to explore their surroundings and stay safely close to you. And it's a lot more fun to walk a calm, polite dog than a dog who's always trying to pull away!

WHAT YOU'LL NEED

▷ Your dog's walking tools (four- to six-foot leash, harness, martingale collar, etc.)

▷ A sandwich bag or pouch of kibble/dry food or other low-value training treats (see page 20)

STEP 1

First, you'll want to practice teaching your dog leash manners inside, where there are fewer distractions than there are outside. Clip their leash onto their collar.

STEP 2

Decide if you want to walk your dog on your right side or your left side to start.

If you choose your right side, position your hands on the leash so your right hand is along the leash closer to your dog, and your left hand holds the handle of the leash. Your right arm should hang straight down at your side, and your left hand by your left hip. Leave enough slack on the leash to form a gentle U-shape. You can wrap any extra leash around your left hand—just make sure to keep the U-shape.

If you choose your left side, follow these directions using the opposite hands and placement. ▷

STEP 3

Begin with your dog in a calm, still position. Take one step forward and wait for a loose leash with no pressure or pulling on the leash from your dog or you. If your dog follows along with you and the leash is still loose, reward them with your "Nice!" or "Yes!" marker word, and a piece of kibble or treat. Keep going, one step at a time, for 10 steps. Reward your dog each time they walk with you without pulling.

STEP 4

Practice this skill once a day inside for five minutes or less. Work on this until your dog can do the 10 steps in a row without any pulling.

After you reach this goal, start rewarding your pup less frequently. Now give them a treat for every three steps you take while still having a loose leash. When you and your dog can walk around your home without pulling, start practicing outside. Have an adult join you if you think it will help.

TIPS

PROBLEM SOLVING

- Don't pull your dog back to correct them if they walk ahead or pull away. Instead, give two light tugs on the leash to get their attention. This will signal to them to release the tension. If they move back toward you and there is no tension on the leash from either you or your dog, reward them.

- Encourage your dog to stay close to your side by holding your treat hand right next to your thigh. Your dog will learn that staying by your side is the best way to get a reward!

- If your dog seems too excited to focus on this training trick, tire them out first with some playtime!

- If you are introducing a new walking tool like a harness to help you manage the pulling, allow your dog to get comfortable with wearing the walking tool without the leash first. Give them lots of treats and playtime while they wear their new gear for a few minutes.

- Even if your dog will only use a collar and leash, let them practice wearing both without anyone holding the leash before you go for a walk.

- For the first few walks, have an adult supervise. Distractions such as people, cars, or other animals can cause your dog to suddenly pull forward, backward, or sideways. You can use the two-handed leash method for more control, but if you have a grown-up with you, they can help if an emergency arises.

- Once you know that you can handle the dog and that they listen to you, ask your grown-up if you can walk your dog by yourself. 🐾

SAFETY

Some dogs have never been taught to walk on a leash before. Puppies will be learning this for the first time. The tension of the leash can make them nervous. If your dog does not want to move while wearing their leash, don't force them or pull them along.

GETTING ALONG WITH OTHER HOUSEHOLD PETS

Dogs may be the world's friendliest creature. They tend to love everyone and they want everyone to love them. Unfortunately, other household pets don't always feel the same way, so first-time introductions are really important for creating lifelong positive relationships between the pets in your home.

WHAT YOU'LL NEED

▷ A leash

▷ A small container of high-value treats

▷ A baby gate (optional)

Note: This lesson is broken down into two parts. Part 1 introduces your new dog to a cat. Part 2 introduces your new dog to a dog.

PART 1: INTRODUCING A CAT

STEP 1

You may not need to introduce your dog to a caged pet like a hamster or a guinea pig, but if you are introducing your dog to a household cat, put a leash on your new dog before bringing them into the house for the first time.

STEP 2

Walk your dog into the home and allow them to sniff around. Your dog will know there's a cat in the house without seeing them. Holding the leash, follow your dog through the house, allowing them to sniff and explore.

STEP 3

When your dog and cat meet for the first time, don't be surprised if the cat runs away immediately. Always allow the cat space to leave the room or hide. Your dog might show interest by perking their ears forward, tilting their head, standing tall at attention, and wagging their tail. These are normal dog responses. Praise your dog and offer them a treat. If your dog cries in excitement, pulls at the leash, or tries to chase the cat, hold the leash firmly, and give a quick, stern "NO."

If your dog responds to your command, praise them and give them a treat.

STEP 4

It will take more than one interaction for your pets to get used to each other. Mostly, this is an exercise in patience. That's when a baby gate can come in handy. Using a baby gate to section off parts of the house will allow your cat to feel more comfortable with approaching your dog through the gate, even once your dog is off the leash and allowed to roam the house freely.

PART 2: INTRODUCING A DOG

STEP 1

Introducing your new dog to another canine household member works a little differently. In this case, you'll want to introduce the dogs off your property, such as at a park. This way, your other dog won't become protective of their home. Following the steps on page 46, have another family member walk one dog while you walk the other, getting closer and watching for their behavior. Once the two dogs are comfortable together, you can bring both dogs home and let them enter the home.

TIPS

PROBLEM SOLVING

• Don't worry if neither pet seems thrilled on the first meeting. It will take some time before your cat and dog get used to each other. Two (or more) dogs will need time to adjust as well. Make sure you're always present when two dogs that don't know each other are together. 🐾

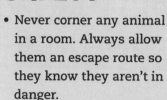

SAFETY

• Never corner any animal in a room. Always allow them an escape route so they know they aren't in danger.

• Don't allow your dog to lunge at a cat. Dogs often want to "play" with other animals, but cats don't always feel the same way. If your dog gets too close, they could hurt the cat (especially an older cat or a kitten) or the cat could hurt them.

• If you have caged pets like small rodents, you'll want to be aware of your dog's location if you handle the rodent outside of the cage. Your dog won't always understand the difference between a hamster and a squeaky toy. So, to keep your rodent safe, don't take them out of the cage while your dog is present.

• Never allow your dog to chase a cat. The cat will come out when they're ready.

PREPARING FOR VET AND GROOMER VISITS

This skill will help your dog stay calm and safe when your vet or groomer handles them to take an X-ray, give a shot, or clip their nails.

WHAT YOU'LL NEED

- ▷ **A few different grooming brushes (rubber grooming glove, bristled brush)**
- ▷ **A towel**
- ▷ **A metal spoon**
- ▷ **A dog toothbrush with a long handle**
- ▷ **A small container of high-value treats and rewards**
- ▷ **An adult to supervise/help**

STEP 1

During playtime or cuddle time, pet and scratch different parts of your dog—on their head, under their chin, and on their neck, back, and sides. After a few days, when your dog gets used to the petting and scratching, start to slowly pet the tops of their paws, lightly stroke their tail, and lightly scratch their ears. When your dog allows you to pet a new part of their body without pulling or turning away from you, use your marker word "Yes!" or "Nice!" and reward them with a high-value treat. Practice this for just a few minutes each day.

STEP 2

After your dog is comfortable being petted all over, start to pet them with different objects. Try giving them a massage with a towel. Use different brushes for a couple of minutes each day—use one brush, then try another, and another. Gently graze the top of their nose and sides of their muzzle (the furry area around their mouth and nose) with the dog toothbrush. Pretend you are a vet using a stethoscope, and gently run a metal spoon across their chest and belly. Every time your dog lets you touch them with a new object, use the marker word to praise them and give them a high-value treat.

STEP 3

After you have practiced this for several days, and your dog is used to being touched in all the different ways, you can begin to handle more sensitive areas, such as their paw and teeth. You may want to have an adult with you to help and make sure your dog is staying calm. Begin by gently wrapping your hand around their paw. When you and your adult helper feel ready and your dog is very calm, you can gently handle their muzzle to brush their teeth.

TIPS

PROBLEM SOLVING

If your dog is too wiggly to stay in place for petting and massages, help them get rid of all that extra energy with a good long playtime. (Making time to play and wear out your dog is also a good idea before taking your dog to a groomer or vet.) 🐾

SAFETY

Pay close attention to your dog's body language when trying to handle them. Here are some signs that your dog is not ready and you need to give them space:

- Their eyes look wider than usual.
- They are yawning a lot.
- They are tucking their tail between their legs.
- They are growling low and quietly.

If any of these things happen, stop and take a break. If you try to force your dog to be touched when they're not ready, they may nip or bite to make you understand they are not happy.

You can help your dog get comfortable while making sure everyone is safe by using a muzzle. When you first try the muzzle, you can load the front of it up with peanut butter or high-value treats.

STOPPING UNNECESSARY BARKING

While it is important for dogs to be able to communicate with us, continuous barking can become a nuisance and heighten your dog's emotions, making them more excitable or more anxious. You will work with your dog to ask them to quiet down while redirecting their attention to a different task.

WHAT YOU'LL NEED

▷ A small container of high-value treats

▷ A leash when teaching a dog to stop barking at the door while you are home, or outside

▷ An additional person to answer the door

Learn this first: "Sit" *(page 52)*

PART 1: BARKING DUE TO EXCITEMENT

STEP 1

It is common for a dog to bark excitedly when someone familiar approaches your home or your yard. Start the exercise by stepping outside of your home for a short time (about one to two minutes).

STEP 2

Be sure that upon returning, have treats at the ready! As your dog is barking when you approach the door, wait until they have quieted down before entering.

STEP 3

As soon as they have stopped barking, enter calmly and reward your dog with the treats while saying "Quiet Down" in an upbeat but calm voice. Give your dog a simple command, such as "Sit," so they will focus their mind on another task. Reward with affection.

STEP 4

Keep practicing over short periods of time before increasing the duration to 10, 20, 30 minutes, and eventually a few hours. Everyone in the household should practice this with your dog.

PART 2: BARKING AT STRANGERS

STEP 1

Many dogs will bark when the unfamiliar scent of a new person or animal approaches their home. Start with your dog's leash attached to them. It helps if you practice this exercise when you know a delivery person or someone unfamiliar to your dog will be approaching your door.

STEP 2

Your pup may not notice that someone has approached the door until there is a knock or a doorbell ring. As soon as your dog begins to bark at the door, calmly walk up to them with a treat in your hand and get their attention. Say "Quiet Down," letting your dog know that you heard their alert and that you do not need them to bark. If they stop barking at the sound of your command, give them a treat.

STEP 3

Pick up the leash and walk your dog to a safe space like their crate. Ask them to perform a simple command, like "Sit," and reward them with positive attention. While you are leading your dog away from the door, your helper can answer the door.

TIPS

GOOD TO KNOW

- Never yell at a dog to "Quiet Down" or "Be Quiet." Yelling or raising your voice will sound like barking to them and will heighten whatever they are feeling in that moment (excitement, alertness, fear).

SAFETY

Pay close attention to your dog's body language. If your dog is showing you signs that they are fearful while barking, have an adult assist you in moving them away. If your dog is barking at you in this manner, they are telling you to give them space and keep away.

BEING OKAY IN A CRATE

A crate or other confinement (carrier, playpen, baby gate) can become a place of comfort and security for your dog. This will come in handy when traveling in a car or airplane, staying in a pet-friendly hotel, during large family gatherings or parties in your home, or when delivery or repair people come to your home. A crate or other confinement can also help with potty training.

WHAT YOU'LL NEED

▷ An appropriately sized crate or small gated area

▷ An old T-shirt or thin towel that smells like you inside the space

▷ A rubber toy that you can fill with peanut butter or a crunchy dog biscuit

▷ A small container of high-value treats, such as plain boiled chicken breast (for other ideas, see page 20)

▷ Low-value treats, such as your dog's kibble/dry food (for other ideas, see page 20)

STEP 1

Before you start, close the crate door. Guide your dog into the room. If they move toward the crate, use a marker word like "Nice!" or "Yes!" and offer them a piece of kibble or other low-value treat. As they get closer to the crate, or sniff the crate, offer them two pieces of kibble. Over time, the dog will make a positive connection between the reward and the crate.

STEP 2

Once your dog is comfortable around the crate, open the crate door. If they sniff inside the crate, reward them with your marker word and drop a piece of kibble inside the crate. As they sniff around, mark each of their efforts with your marker word and drop pieces of kibble into the crate. The more often your dog enters the crate, increase the number of kibble that you offer them.

STEP 3

When your dog is fully inside of the crate, offer them a high-value treat and lots of praise—"Good dog!" If they stay inside the crate or enter it again, offer another high-value treat, and then another. If your dog seems nervous in the crate, don't force them to stay inside. Give them some space and try again later.

STEP 4

As soon as your dog is comfortable being inside of the crate, place their rubber toy inside with them. Calmly close the crate door. You want to make the crate a calm place where they want to be.

STEP 5

After a minute or two, open the crate door without ceremony and calmly walk away from the crate. Until your dog learns the "Stay" command (page 74), let them leave the crate whenever they're ready. Give your dog lots of affection and kibble or other low-value treats for a job well done! The next time you practice this skill with your dog, you can increase the amount of time they spend in the cage (see problem solving tip). ▶

TIPS

GOOD TO KNOW

Some dogs experience severe separation anxiety even without being confined! This can happen even when they are left alone for short periods of time. This anxiety can lead to destructive behavior, property damage, or worse, your dog harming themselves. If this happens, talk with your grown-up and veterinarian. The vet may be able to offer medication, supplements, or behavioral therapy to calm their anxiety.

PROBLEM SOLVING

• Your dog may whine or bark once the crate door is closed (Step 4) and they're finished with their special toy. Let them calm themselves by offering positive marker words like "Nice!" or "Yes!" From the moment they are quiet, count 30 seconds to yourself. If they can stay quiet for 30 seconds, drop a high-value treat into the crate. If they continue to whine, you can open the crate. If they stay calm and quiet, repeat the 30-second count and treat. Do this three times. After this, you can increase the time to 60 seconds, followed by a treat. Do this three times. (Then you can increase the time by two minutes, then five minutes, and finally 10 minutes, each done three times.) At any time, if your dog continues to whine, let them out of the crate with a reassurance such as "It's okay," but offer no treat.

• Another way to help your dog adjust to the crate is by feeding meals inside of it. As soon as they finish eating, remove the dish and offer them a high-value treat or toy to entertain them in the crate until it is time to go potty.

- Your dog may need to be convinced to enter the crate. Place their extra special toy into the crate to lure them inside. Once they're inside, offer them encouraging words and high-value treats as you close the crate.

- If your dog is having difficulty being quiet while in their crate, work with whatever their longest amount of time is—even if it's just 30 seconds—and try that for up to 10 repetitions. End training for the day, and try again the next day. The next day, time your dog starting with the longest amount of quiet time they did the day before, and increase from there.

SAFETY

- Don't force a dog into a crate or use a crate as punishment. The crate should be a training space and a happy place.

- Never leave a dog in a crate for longer than four hours at a time, except when sleeping overnight. Dogs need to be able to stretch their legs, move around, and play!

- Dogs that bite, scratch, or pull at the crate bars, or show anxious body language (i.e., shaking, panting, drooling, intense barking) for longer than 10 minutes can hurt themselves. If your dog does any of these things, end the exercise patiently and start over the next day. If you don't see much improvement over the following week, you may need to decide on a different type of confinement.

BEING HOUSEBROKEN (AKA POTTY TRAINING)

Potty training a dog is a great achievement for your dog and for you! Your dog is learning the rules of your home and that there is a place for everything—including their pee and poop. You can teach them when and where it is okay to use the bathroom by:

1. *Keeping a regular feeding and potty schedule, and*
2. *Paying attention to your dog's signals.*

WHAT YOU'LL NEED

▷ **Walk Schedule & Potty Chart (page 153)**

▷ **Pen**

▷ **Paper (optional)**

▷ **A crate**

▷ **Your dog's walking equipment (leash and any extras you may need, such as a harness, martingale collar, etc.)**

▷ **Poop scoop/poop bags**

▷ **Potty pads (for puppies who are not yet fully vaccinated)**

▷ **A sandwich bag or pouch of kibble/dry food or low-value training treats**

STEP 1

If you or your grown-up don't have access to a scanner or copy machine to make copies of the Walk Schedule & Potty Chart, you can simply create one by copying page 153 using a pen and paper. The schedule will help your dog's body learn when it's time to go potty (see Good to Know tip). The chart will keep track of when they did number one and two and will help you see patterns in your dog's bathroom habits, like how many times a day they usually need to poop.

STEP 2

The first bathroom trip for your dog is their wake-up bathroom trip. They've been inside all night and probably have to "go" as soon as they wake up. Go to your dog's crate or space, clip on their leash, and walk outside quickly but safely. You don't have to run—actually, running might cause them to poop early!

STEP 3

When you have arrived at an appropriate space, like a nice patch of grass that's out of the way from where people walk, let your dog sniff around for a spot where they want to relieve themselves. If your dog does not pee or poop within three minutes, walk them to a new spot a few feet away. As soon as your dog is finished peeing or pooping (or both!), reward them with their kibble and lots of verbal praise. If you think they will do more, walk them farther along to another potty spot. Reward them again as soon as they are finished.

STEP 4

Don't forget to scoop the poop! Prevent illnesses and dirty potty spots by using poop bags to grab and tie up the poop, and toss it in an outdoor garbage can. ▶

STEP 5

Make a note in the Walk Schedule & Potty Chart of what time your dog peed and pooped. You will probably feed your dog right after their wake-up bathroom break, and they will need to go out again after this meal. See the following tip for how to schedule bathroom breaks, since it depends on your dog's age and other factors.

TIPS

GOOD TO KNOW

- The age of your dog or puppy will help you decide how many hours should be between bathroom breaks. Puppies need to go potty more often—it may be good to start with bathroom breaks every hour or two. You will begin to get an idea of how often they actually go when you take them. Older dogs can often go several hours between bathroom breaks. All dogs need to use the bathroom first thing in the morning, in the afternoon, and after dinner/before bedtime. The type of dog food you offer can also affect how often your dog goes.

- Once your dog has settled on a potty spot, try to use this same area for future bathroom breaks. Dogs don't like to poop in dirty areas, so that's another good reason to clean up their poop each time they go.

- When you are adjusting your dog to their new schedule, take them out again 15 minutes after their first meal. They should go out after every meal. As you get to know your dog's habits, you may need to adjust their schedule.

PROBLEM SOLVING
Some signs that your dog needs to go out might include:

- Standing by the door
- Scratching at the door

- Circling or pacing
- Whining
- Sniffing
- Coming to you, whining or wagging
- Moving into a corner

Even if you stick to a schedule, accidents happen. Adult dogs may have accidents when they are scared, feeling sick, or getting older. If you see your dog showing signs of wanting to go potty inside, try to distract them by making an excitable sound, showing them a toy, or using a high-value treat. Even if they start to go on the floor, leash them up and take them outside so they can finish in their regular spot. When they go outside, praise and reward them.

If you find evidence of an accident (like a puddle on the floor), don't scold or get upset with your dog. They will not make the connection that you are upset about something that happened in the past and will become scared. Scolding them or making them look at the mess they made can result in your dog trying to "hide" the evidence by eating it to avoid a future scolding. Calmly clean up the accident with an enzymatic cleaner (you can buy this online or in a pet store) to eliminate all traces and smells. This will reduce the chance of them having another accident in the same spot. You may need to adjust your dog's Walk Schedule by adding more potty breaks when needed.

PUPPY

If your puppy has not received all their vaccinations, you'll want to practice their potty schedule on potty pads either inside of the home or on clean pavement. You can still use a leash to guide them, just like you would outside. 🐾

SAFETY

- Always have your dog on a leash when you take them outside for bathroom walks, even in your yard. This way, you can keep an eye on their bathroom habits and clean up their poop, keeping their area as sanitary as possible.

- When scooping up your dog's poop, have one hand holding the leash to keep your dog close and the other hand using a poop bag to scoop. If you need help doing both, you can bring your dog in and return outside to pick up the poop, or have a grown-up help you with bathroom walks until you get the hang of things.

HAVING GOOD MANNERS AROUND OTHER DOGS

Dogs are pack animals, and the people they live with are their primary pack members! If dogs aren't introduced to other dogs properly, they may view their own kind as something to be afraid of. Learn how to introduce your pet to other dogs early on, so they learn how to make friends. This will help them view dogs as pack members, too, and this can be lots of fun!

WHAT YOU'LL NEED

▷ A leash

▷ A small container of high-value treats

▷ A friend with a dog

▷ Adult supervision

▷ A neutral location (somewhere that doesn't "belong" to either dog)

STEP 1

Ask an adult to go with you for dog introductions. Make a plan to meet a friend and their dog, maybe at a local park. Don't meet at either dog's house or yard. This can make that dog feel "in charge" or protective. With each dog on a firmly held leash, you and your friend can walk your dogs 10 to 20 feet away from each other. Walk in the same direction, but don't let the dogs go near each other yet. If your dog stays calm and happy, reward them with a treat. If your dog looks at the other dog with interest, you can reward them with a happy "Good dog!" and give them a treat.

STEP 2

If the dogs are relaxed and comfortable, get a little closer. Offer praise and treats each time they look at each other without any defensive behavior. If either dog becomes defensive, increase the distance between the dogs. Defensive behaviors include:

• Hair standing up on the dog's back
• Teeth-baring
• Growling
• Staring that you can't break

STEP 3

Let the dogs determine how quickly or slowly they want to get together. Some dogs are comfortable right away and will be friends from the start. Others need more time. Once you're able to walk side by side with your friend, walk your dogs together and continue to watch for any signs of stress or aggression in either dog.

STEP 4

After your leashed dogs have behaved nicely near each other several times, you are certain they get along, and an adult agrees they are ready to be introduced off leash, you may introduce them to each other in an enclosed yard. Remove any toys or treats, as these can cause a fight.

TIPS

PROBLEM SOLVING

- Remember, your dog isn't the only dog being introduced to someone new. Your friend's dog is excited, too. Take time to introduce and watch both animals slowly and carefully. A rushed introduction can ruin a relationship for life.

- Allow the Doggie "Handshake" to happen. When humans say hello, we often do it with a wave or a handshake, but dogs don't have hands, so they use their noses. Dogs will often sniff each other all over to learn about the other dog. That's totally normal. Yes, even when they sniff each other's privates. That's just a dog's way of saying hi! (Thank goodness humans don't do this!) 🐾

SAFETY

- Never force dogs who don't get along to stay together. Some dogs won't get along no matter what.

- Make sure that you and your friend hold your leashes firmly. Even if they like each other, your dogs will be excited, and excited dogs are strong! Have your dog under control at all times.

- If your dog pulls the leash from your hand, or the animals begin to fight, never get between them. Let the supervising adult handle the dogs. A fearful or aggressive dog might not mean to bite you, but they won't always be able to control themselves in the middle of a stressful situation.

③

BASIC COMMANDS

Basic commands are words that will help you communicate with your dog and tell them what you want them to do. Most of these commands are behaviors that your dog already does. For example, your dog already knows how to sit. You will teach them the word for sit—and eventually they will learn that "Sit" means that they should sit! Basic commands are a fun way to engage with your dog and learn together. We'll also take commands one step further by attaching hand signals. This way, you and your dog will develop even stronger communication skills with each other.

"TOUCH"

"Touch" simply means that you want your dog to touch something. This command is an easy way to help your dog learn to trust you and make them understand that your hand is not a threat. This command helps teach your dog to direct their focus on you, especially when they are off their leash. "Touch" also teaches your dog to *target* specific objects. We'll use this command to teach them more challenging tricks later, too.

ITEMS NEEDED

▷ A small, quiet room without distractions

▷ A leash (for when it's time to practice outside)

▷ A sandwich bag or pouch of kibble or dry dog food

You can use low-value, low-calorie treats (see ideas on page 20) if your dog eats wet food.

You can use high-value treats (see ideas on page 20) if your dog is shy and needs more encouragement.

STEP 1

Keeping your treat hand in a fist behind your back, gently hold out the palm of your other hand to your dog. As your dog investigates and touches your hand with their nose, use your marker word "Nice!" or "Yes!" and give them a treat from your treat hand.

STEP 2

Put your empty hand behind your back with your treat hand and wait a couple of seconds, then repeat Step 1. Repeat Step 1 successfully 10 times in a row before moving on to the next step. If your dog is not able to do this step, they may need a play break.

STEP 3

This time, wait one second and then offer your empty hand and say in an even, strong (but not forceful) voice, "Touch." This will help your dog start to understand what you are asking them to do when they hear this command. Use your marker word "Nice!" or "Yes!" and reward your dog with kibble or a high-value treat.

STEP 4

Repeat Step 3 using the word "Touch" 10 times. Work on this command every day in different spaces. As they get the hang of it, slowly increase the space between you and your dog. Eventually, you can move this activity outside, with an adult close by. When you do this exercise outside, keep your dog's leash clipped onto them, and practice until they respond to your command without hesitating or getting distracted. Reward with marker words and treats.

TIPS

PROBLEM SOLVING

If you have a very shy dog, try offering your hand with your palm facing down and your body facing away from your dog. This will make you seem less scary or threatening. Try making yourself as small and nonthreatening to your dog as possible—you can even sit on the ground. Use a quieter, even tone of voice when telling your dog to "Touch."

PUPPY

If your puppy is teething and chooses to chew on your hand instead of just touching, you can use Basic Training Lesson "Taking Treats Gently" (page 27), where you teach your pup to gently take treats from your hand. 🐾

SAFETY

Keep your treat hand behind your back until they follow the command. You want your dog to focus on touching their nose to your free hand instead of your treat hand.

"SIT"

This basic but awesome command will teach your dog how to greet people politely and wait patiently. Your dog is learning self-control, which will help them stop what they are doing and wait for your directions. They may be excited that they're getting a treat, but with practice, they will learn that the treat won't come until they sit patiently!

ITEMS NEEDED

▷ A small container of high-value treats

▷ A quiet place with no distractions

STEP 1

Place a piece of treat into your treat hand and make a fist around it. Let your dog sniff your hand so they know you have a treat for them.

STEP 2

Without touching your dog, move your closed treat hand from in front of your dog's nose, up their snout, to just over their eyebrows. Be patient and don't open your hand. In order to keep their eyes on the prize, your dog will slowly figure out that they should sit.

STEP 3

When your dog sits back all the way and does not pop right back up, use your marker word "Nice!" or "Yes!" and give them the treat. Practice this five times in a row, or until your dog can sit back each time.

STEP 4

Once you can do Step 3 over and over, you are now ready to add in the word "Sit." As your dog gets ready to sit back, say "Sit" once in a clear and strong voice (without being forceful). If they follow the command, reward them with the marker word and treat. Practice with the word "Sit" five times in a row before ending your training session. Eventually, you will be able to give treats less often, and finally, you will be able to use your hand as you did in Step 2 without even needing a treat.

TIPS

PROBLEM SOLVING

- If you hold the treat too far from your dog's nose or too high above their eyes, they will try to follow the treat by moving forward or jumping up. If you hold the treat too low, your dog will move backward so they can see the treat hand clearly.

- Even once they're trained, it's not easy to get dogs to sit when they are excited, like when you come home from a long day at school. If your dog jumps up when you ask them to sit, turn your body away, and stand firm. Ignore your dog until they are calm. Ask them to "Sit" in a firm and even voice, and reward them with chin scratches and affection only once they are seated and have all four paws on the floor. ▶

PUPPY

Puppies have a hard time learning this command because they end up in what I call a "puppy slide," which is more like lying down. You can help teach your puppy how to hold a sitting position by having them practice with a wall or solid surface behind them. You can also position them by putting one hand behind their back knees and the other hand on their chest, gently tucking them into a sitting position. 🐾

"CHECK"

"Check" is all about eye contact, and eye contact helps build trust with your dog. It also refocuses their attention on you when you need them to. In the animal world, direct eye contact can be considered threatening or aggressive. But if you teach your dog "Check," they will learn that looking at you and other people is a good thing, as people mean dogs no harm! "Check" can be very useful on walks for city dogs who may get easily distracted.

ITEMS NEEDED

▷ A bag or pouch of low-value treats

Learn this first: "Sit" (page 52) and "Wait" (page 66). The dog should also have good self-control skills.

STEP 1

Sit on the floor in front of your dog. Command your dog to "Sit" as well. Have a treat in your fist and hold it out to them. Allow them to sniff it.

STEP 2

Raise your treat hand up to your nose, in between your eyes. When your dog's focus goes from the treat hand to your eyes, make eye contact and give your dog the treat. Repeat this lesson 10 times in a row successfully. ▶

STEP 3

This time, hold your treat hand behind your back. Use your free hand to point to your nose and say "Check." Once your dog looks at your eyes, and is not looking for your treat hand, mark the behavior with "Yes!" or "Nice!" and give your dog their treat. Repeat this lesson 10 times successfully.

STEP 4

Repeat Step 3, but increase the amount of time that your dog holds eye contact with you to three seconds before giving their treat. With practice, your dog should be able to hold eye contact with you for five seconds.

STEP 5

Before using "Check" outside while on walks, try practicing indoors with your dog on a leash as you walk around your home together. Try teaching "Check" in the kitchen when there are delicious smells cooking!

TIPS

PROBLEM SOLVING

If your dog doesn't make eye contact with you when your treat hand is behind you, try calling their name in a firm and confident tone and follow their name with the "Check" command. 🐾

"HEEL"

"Heel" means stay next to you. It is good manners for your dog to stay next to you when walking and not cross in front of or behind you, or worse, walk or run ahead of you. The "Heel" command makes walks, on a leash and off, safer and more enjoyable. If your dog knows the hand motions from "Touch" and "Check," then teaching them "Heel" will be easy to build upon.

ITEMS NEEDED

▷ A bag or pouch of low-value treats

▷ Your dog suited up in their walking gear (leash and any other walking tools)

Learn this first: "Touch" (page 50) and "Check" (page 55)

STEP 1

Begin in a quiet space without distractions. Have proper hand placement on the leash (see page 29), with your dog to your preferred side. Keep treats out of sight in a hand or pocket away from your dog. ▶

STEP 2

Walk four steps forward with your dog next to you. If they pull ahead or pull back, stop moving. Adjust your position so your leash isn't tight.

STEP 3

Tell your dog "Check" so they look at you. Now place your hand down at your side right next to your knee as though you were asking for "Touch" (page 50), but do not say the word "Touch."

STEP 4

When your dog walks back and puts their nose next to your knee, say "Heel." When they are next to you, you can give them a treat, but make sure your treat hand is pressed against your knee. This teaches your dog that they will only get the treat if they stay close to you.

STEP 5

Repeat until you can walk four steps with your dog next to you. When your dog can do this, jackpot them with your marker word and multiple treats! Repeat this lesson, increasing the number of steps you walk before rewarding them.

STEP 6

Get your dog to "Heel" faster by giving them more treats or affection when they move back to your side quickly.

TIPS

PROBLEM SOLVING

If your dog is shy and usually keeps their distance from you during walks, try these tips:

- Use high-value treats.
- Go at their pace to help them feel more confident with you.
- Be patient.

PUPPY

Wait to teach a puppy "Heel" until they are comfortable walking on a leash. The sudden tension of the leash can startle them. You want to create a positive and fun learning experience for your pup!

SAFETY

When you practice "Heel" with your dog in a new place, keep them on their leash. New smells and distractions can make it too hard for your dog to focus on you, and they may try to run off and explore their new surroundings.

"DOWN"

"Down" is the command for a dog to lie down and teaches your dog good manners by putting them in the resting position. When a dog's body is in a resting position, it's easier for them to calm their mind as well. Think about it—don't you feel more relaxed when you are lying down? Your dog does, too!

ITEMS NEEDED

▷ High-value treats in both hands

▷ A blanket or towel for your dog to lie on, preferably one they already use

Learn this first: "Sit" (page 52)

STEP 1

Lay the blanket or towel down for your dog. Put small pieces of high-value treats into both of your hands and make them into fists. Place one hand behind your back. Using the other hand to demonstrate that you have a treat, lure and call your dog over to the blanket.

STEP 2

Tell your dog to "Sit" on the blanket or towel. Once they are in a steady sit position, kneel down to get closer to your dog's level.

STEP 3

Just like you did with the "Sit" command, hold one of your treat hands close to your dog's nose. Slowly move your hand down in a straight line toward the floor or their toes. This technique is called "nose to toes." The goal is for your dog's head to follow your hand into a lying down position. Your pup may lick at your treat hand as they move downward; this is okay. Once they lie, use a marker word and give them a treat—not from the front hand, but from the hand that was behind your back. Practice this exercise five times.

STEP 4

Now repeat the exercise using the word "Down" just like when you taught your dog "Sit." Each day, make your dog lie in the "Down" position a little bit longer before rewarding them with your marker word and treat. Once they have mastered "Down" while you are kneeling, begin practicing "Down" while you are standing up. ▶

Next, do the hand luring gesture without any treats in the luring hand and without going all the way down to the ground. The less you use treats as a reward, the more you can use affection and petting as the prize.

TIPS

PROBLEM SOLVING

- It is much easier to teach a dog "Down" after they know how to do "Sit" without always expecting a treat. Some dogs will pop right back up in a sitting or standing position as soon as they lie down on command. Try rewarding them for simply lying down for a while when you're not in the middle of a lesson. Casually walk over to them, use your marker word, and give them a treat. When you practice the "Down" training sessions, they will start to make the connection that only when they stay in a lying down position will they receive a reward.

- It's important to practice "Down" in different spaces and on different surfaces. Some dogs need their security blanket or towel to remember that they can perform the command in a different setting. So, if you are trying to teach your dog "Down" on a driveway or a grassy surface, start by practicing with their towel or blanket on the driveway or grass, and then use it less often over the next week.

- When a dog is following the lure downward, their backside may go up in the air like in a downward dog yoga position. Sorry, doggie, that's only half down! Have a helper with you if your dog usually does this. Your helper can gently push your dog's backside downward (if your dog is okay with this) while you slowly pull the treat toward you, keeping your hand along the floor. Your dog's body should naturally lie out on the ground as their nose keeps reaching for your luring hand. 🐾

"DROP IT"

"Drop It" is used when a dog has something in their mouth that we want them to release, so we don't have to use our hands to take something out of the dog's mouth. This command will be helpful in teaching them more advanced tricks later, such as fetch (page 133), and make these tricks more fun.

ITEMS NEEDED

▷ A low-value toy or item

▷ A high-value toy or item

▷ A small container of high-value treats for Steps 5 and 6

Note: This lesson is broken down into two parts. The first part teaches a dog to drop something. The second part teaches a dog to drop something as a trade for something else.

PART 1: "DROP IT"

STEP 1

Using a toy, play with your dog for 10 to 20 seconds. Wrap your hands around part of the toy so your dog can't put the whole toy in their mouth.

STEP 2

Stop playing and hold on to the toy until your dog gets bored and lets go of it. The moment your dog takes their mouth off the toy, reward them with your marker word and affection. Start playing again, and repeat this lesson five more times.

STEP 3

Play again. This time, the second your dog removes their mouth from the toy, say "Drop It." When they look at you, mark and reward their behavior! Repeat this lesson 10 times.

STEP 4

Adjust your grip on the toy so you are holding less of it in your hands, and repeat the lesson. With practice, you will be able to ask your dog to drop a toy even if you're not holding it. ▶

PART 2: "DROP IT" FOR A TRADE

STEP 5

Once you dog masters "Drop It," you can also teach "Drop It" by trading. This is helpful if your dog gets hold of something they aren't supposed to have. Make a fist around a high-value treat. Hold your fist to your dog, letting them sniff your hand.

STEP 6

Say the command "Drop It." As your dog opens their mouth to release the object, give them the high-value treat. With the other hand, remove the forbidden object from your dog.

TIPS

PROBLEM SOLVING

Dogs are clever. If your dog makes a game out of grabbing things they should not have and running away, you can be clever, too, and change the game. Make yourself and another object or treat much more exciting than whatever your dog has. Act happy and excited about the dog dropping their item and taking a new, better one. Don't chase or panic if your dog runs off with the item. Your dog will get confused, either thinking they should protect what they have and keep it away from you or that you are playing with them. 🐾

SAFETY

Only an adult whom the dog trusts should try to remove an item from a dog's mouth. Otherwise, use a very high-value treat to tempt the dog to release the dangerous item. Some dogs may show signs of "resource guarding." This is when a dog tries to protect items in their possession. Resource guarding can make teaching "Drop It" harder, but not impossible.

Some dogs show signs of severe resource guarding. Don't approach a dog who is showing these signs, and tell an adult:

- Their body will stiffen.
- The hair on the back of their neck will stand up.
- They may look away entirely or look at you with what looks like a side eye.
- They may growl or snarl.

"WAIT"

"Wait" is another self-control exercise that teaches patience and reminds dogs about the need for good manners. This command helps reinforce your dog's ability to gently take food, treats, and toys from your hand and to show good behavior when waiting for meals. Your dog does not have to sit during this exercise, but they should be calm and still, and have all paws on the floor.

ITEMS NEEDED

▷ A bag or pouch of kibble/low-value treats

▷ A small container of high-value treats

▷ A favorite toy

▷ A food dish with a small amount of dog food (to do this at mealtime)

Learn this first: "Off" (page 72)

STEP 1

While your dog is sitting or standing still, hold a piece of low-value treat in a fist behind your back. Calmly extend your treat hand, in a fist, straight out in front of you at your shoulder height.

STEP 2

For five seconds, slowly lower your fist of the treats to your dog's nose.

STEP 3

If your dog tries to jump up, or reach for your treat hand before you finish lowering, say "Off" and pull the treat away. Hide your treat hand behind your back again. When your dog's paws are back on the ground, start over from Step 1.

STEP 4

When your dog can wait patiently as you lower your hand, reward them with your marker word and the treat. Do this exercise five times. Next, increase the amount of time lowering your hand to 10 seconds.

Do this five times. You can stop and try again later or another day if your dog loses focus. The goal is to be able to do this for 15 seconds. Now you can use this command for high-value treats, food at mealtimes, and their toy. Be sure to always praise your dog with your marker word! ▶

TIPS

PROBLEM SOLVING

- Your pup may have lots of energy and continue to jump up or search for their reward even after you hide your treat hand behind your back. If the "Off" command does not work the first time, turn your body away from your dog and don't give them any attention until they have calmed down. Once they are calm, you can try this exercise again.

- With smaller dogs, one may have to kneel down, because starting in a standing position and arm up at shoulder level would be considered too high and entice your dog to jump up in an effort to reach the treat.

PUPPY

Start with your arm at about waist level. For very young puppies or shy dogs, start in a kneeling position so you are smaller and the motion of lowering your hand does not seem as scary. 🐾

"PLACE"

"Place" is kind of like "Stay," but with a specific spot in mind. Teaching your dog "Place" can keep them safe, such as from running out the door when people are entering or leaving your home. It can also help keep your dog from getting nervous or barking at the door, by going to a comfortable space that calms them. This is also helpful when you visit a new place with your dog, as they will connect "Place" with going to a safe, comforting spot.

ITEMS NEEDED

▷ **A leash**

▷ **A blanket or dog bed**

▷ **A small container of high-value treats**

Learn this first: "Touch" (page 50), "Down" (page 60), and "Stay" (page 74). The dog will also need to know their name.

STEP 1

Whether you are inside or out, use a leash when you start teaching your dog "Place." You don't have to hold the leash; you'll only need to pick it up and use it if your dog walks away from the "Place" or needs extra help getting there.

STEP 2

Lay your dog's bed or blanket down while they are watching you. Hopefully the motion of the blanket or bed will interest them enough to walk over to you. If you need to encourage your dog by luring them with a treat, this is okay.

STEP 3

If your pup places a paw or two onto their bed or blanket, use the marker word "Yes!" or "Nice!" and give them a treat. You can also use the command "Touch" with an empty hand over the blanket and have your dog walk onto the blanket. Give a treat from the other hand. Keep repeating this and increase the number of treats you give your dog every time they put more paws on the blanket and stay on longer. Note that every time you repeat this step, make sure to walk your dog away from the blanket to practice teaching them to go onto it. ▷

STEP 4

Once all your dog's paws are on the bed or blanket, use the "Down" command to get them to lie down, followed by "Stay." Treat them for lying and staying on the blanket.

STEP 5

Once your dog has mastered Steps 1 to 4, start to work on the verbal command for "Place." While you have your dog's attention, but they are not on the bed or blanket, make eye contact with them. Stand by the dog bed or blanket, say their name, and point to their bed. Your dog may look at you and seem confused by what you are saying. Give them a few seconds before repeating the command. A successful "Place" is when they walk over to their spot, lie down, and stay lying down. Reward them with a marker word and a treat. After five successful repetitions, you can increase the distance between you and your dog's "Place" when you give this command.

TIPS

GOOD TO KNOW

Remember to only use marker words and reward your pup when they perform the command successfully. Once your dog is skilled following "Place" with their bed or blanket, try teaching them that their crate and any other spot that is comfortable to them could also mean "Place." This will make it much easier to help them settle in new spaces or keep them out of the way when needed.

PROBLEM SOLVING

Your dog may try to pop back up from lying down when you teach them "Place." You can encourage them to stay lying down by giving them a calming chew toy. The longer they stay lying down, the more you can reward them with treats.

PUPPY

Teaching "Place" to a puppy is tricky, especially when they are teething. Puppies will be tempted to chew on blankets and beds. Try practicing with old towels and T-shirts to start. Offer calming teething toys while teaching your puppy "Place." This will help teach them what is appropriate for them to nibble on and what is not.

SAFETY

By keeping a leash on your dog when you teach this trick, you can keep your dog close to their "Place." If they get distracted, bring their attention back to the exercise by picking up the leash and walking them back over closer to their bed or blanket. Once they figure out this skill, you can remove the leash.

If you are teaching this skill outside, always use the leash until your dog can respond to their name by coming back over to you immediately when called, no matter what is going on around them.

"OFF"

The "Off" command is used to tell your dog to get off something, like furniture, or off someone—like your friend, your aunt, or even your grandma! Dogs can jump on something to try and reach an object that smells interesting or to find a new place to curl up on. They may also jump on people they are very excited to see. Teaching this command takes a lot of time and patience because you have to command your dog at the exact time they are doing this behavior, and they may be very excited. But it teaches very important habits, such as self-control and knowledge that they should not climb on things that are off-limits, and that jumping on people can frighten them or even knock them over! The good news is, once you train a dog not to jump, they will generally remember this rule forever.

ITEMS NEEDED

▷ **A small container of high-value treats, stored out of your dog's reach but easy for you to get to**

Learn this first: "Sit" *(page 52)*

STEP 1

Wait for the behavior. When you see your dog putting their paws on the counter or table, or preparing to jump onto furniture that they are not allowed on, stop what you are doing and say "Off" to them in a firm, serious voice (but not yelling). You'll have to act quickly so your dog learns that they will only hear that word when they are doing something they're not supposed to be doing.

STEP 2

Quickly grab that high-value treat and hold it in your fist to lure them. As soon as all four paws are on the floor, you can mark the behavior with a "Nice!" or "Yes!" and give them the treat.

TIPS

GOOD TO KNOW

- Consistency is important. You and your family members must practice this every single time your dog tries to climb or jump on off-limits furniture. You can also use this technique to stop your dog from jumping up at people or onto them. Some people may say, "It's okay, I don't mind," but you can command your dog "Off," and then explain that you are training your dog so they won't jump on anybody. Your dog might get confused if some people let them jump.

- If you clip a leash to your dog, you can help teach and guide your dog off of furniture using the leash. Note that rewards shouldn't be given if you use this method.

PROBLEM SOLVING

Your dog may start to think that every time they jump onto something and hear "Off," they will get a treat. This can backfire, and your dog might then try to jump just to get the treat. You can outsmart this behavior, though! Just follow the "Off" command with "Sit." The "Sit" command will then become connected to the treats and affection. 🐾

SAFETY

If you have a larger or more energetic dog, you may need to use a leash, especially if they are jumping on people. If your dog gets very excited when people enter your home, try keeping a leash clipped onto them if you know company is coming. Before your dog gets close enough to jump on the visitor, grab the leash and walk them away. Tell your dog to "Sit" and keep them at your side. You can then direct the person to walk toward you but ignore the dog. If your dog is able to remain sitting, give them pieces of treats. Once they are calmer, you can invite your visitor to offer their hand for your dog to sniff and then give chin scratches if desired—but only while your dog is in the sitting position.

"STAY"

"Stay" is a tough command for dogs to learn, because it tests their ability to focus no matter how far away you are and how long you want them to stay. Distractions can also make it hard for a dog to focus on this command. But if you teach your dog this skill and practice it in different places, it can actually be a lifesaver! For example, if your dog ever runs off too far and you need them to stop and stay put, the "Stay" command will keep them safe and still until you can get to them.

ITEMS NEEDED

▷ A small container of high-value treats

Learn this first: "Sit" (page 52) and "Stay" (page 74)

Note: *This lesson is broken down into two parts. The first steps will help you train your dog on staying still no matter how far away you are (distance) and how long you want the to stay (duration). The second steps will help you teach your dog to stay even when there are distractions!*

PART 1: DISTANCE AND DURATION

STEP 1

Stand close to your dog and ask them to "Sit." When they're sitting, reward them with your marker word and a treat. Next, give them the hand signal for "Stay," which is a flat hand with your fingers together and facing up to the sky, your thumb just in front of your chest.

STEP 2

After showing your dog the hand signal for "Stay," say the word "Stay" in a strong, clear voice (but not yelling). Look up and straight ahead, away from your dog. Still facing your dog, take one step backward. Stay there for five seconds, without making eye contact with your dog.

STEP 3

Now step back to your starting position without looking at your pup. If they are able to remain sitting while you return to your starting position, make eye contact and reward them with their marker word and well-deserved treat! Once your dog masters this trick, repeat it five times. After this, increase the distance to two steps backward, then three steps. Try to make it to five paces away, holding your position for five seconds, and doing this five times.

STEP 4

Repeat Steps 1 through 3, but now with each step back, increase your time to 10 seconds. If your dog stays, they win a jackpot! Jackpot your dog with two treats, one at a time and a few seconds apart so your dog can chew and you can stand back up after giving each treat. Now increase to 15 seconds, and jackpot with three treats. When you increase your time to 20 seconds, jackpot with four treats. Keep increasing the time until your dog can hold a "Stay" position for 30 seconds while you are five paces away, for five repetitions. And yes, jackpot them with five treats and lots of affection!

PART 2: DISTRACTIONS

STEP 5

Now that you have worked on distance and duration, it is time to challenge your dog with distractions. You will be moving around your dog and making stops along the way. A simple way to picture your path is by thinking of a clock. Imagine that your dog is the center of the clock. When you are standing right in front of your dog, you are at six o'clock. Now take one step to your left, to where seven would be on the face of a clock.

STEP 6

If your dog gets up, use the "Sit" command to put them back into a sitting position while you stay in your position at seven. Once they sit, return to your position at six and take one step to seven. Once you can take one step to seven three times in a row, and wait five ▶

Practice "Stay" inside before moving outside. If you will be practicing in an open space that is enclosed or fenced in, ask an adult to stay with you. Clip a long leash to your dog's collar and use high-value treats to encourage them to focus on you.

seconds each time, you can add one more step and move to eight. You don't have to hold for five seconds in between multiple steps. The purpose is to train your dog to "Stay" while movement is happening around them.

STEP 7

Now walk back two steps to six and face your dog directly. You can release them from "Sit" and "Stay" with a release word like "Okay!" Now jackpot your dog with up to three treats. If they are willing, repeat the exercise, but try to move farther along the clock each time until you can get to eleven.

STEP 8

Once you reach eleven three times in a row, try walking all the way around the clock. Don't stop or turn back. Finish the circle, walking around your dog. If they are able to "Stay" and "Sit" without repositioning them-selves to look at you while you move around them, jackpot them with five treats. If they are able, repeat this exercise five more times.

TIPS

GOOD TO KNOW

Once your dog masters all these steps, each time you practice, make the circle around your dog larger so you increase your distance from them. With practice, you will be able to get them to remain in a "Stay" position for a short time, even when you are completely out of their sight!

PROBLEM SOLVING

When you make eye contact, your dog may mistake that as a signal to move toward you before you say "Okay." Try to avoid eye contact until it is time to give them their treat, and only reward them after you have given them the "Okay" to move from the "Sit" and "Stay" position. 🐾

"LEAVE IT"

"Leave It" means don't touch. This command is used to turn a dog's attention away from a tempting item or snack. This skill can prevent your pup from eating something harmful, like a poisonous food or a choking hazard. "Leave It" can help you avoid emergency trips to the veterinarian!

ITEMS NEEDED

▷ A bag or pouch of low-value treats

▷ A small container of high-value treats

Learn this first: "Wait" (page 66)

STEP 1

Put a low-value treat in one hand and a high-value treat in the other. Make a fist around both treats, and place the fist with the high-value treat behind your back.

STEP 2

Kneel in front of your dog, and hold out the fist with the low-value treat. They may sniff or paw at your hand. The second your dog looks away from the fist, mark the behavior with "Yes!" or "Nice!" and reward them with the high-value treat from behind your back. Repeat this five times before moving on to Step 3.

STEP 3

Add in the verbal command "Leave It." When your dog begins to check out your treat fist, but before they make contact with their nose or paw, say "Leave It." If they either look at you or away from the treat hand, reward them with the treat from behind your back.

STEP 4

Now comes the hard part for your dog! This time, hold your treat hand open, with the back of your hand flat on the floor. Repeat Step 3 and say "Leave It." If your dog gets too close to the treat or ignores your command, close your fist and quickly put it behind your back before they can eat the treat. ▶

Repeat until your dog understands that they must turn their attention completely away from the treat. When they succeed, reward that good dog with praise and a treat! Then repeat this five times.

STEP 5

This next step is tricky, too. Ask a grown-up to supervise. You will need to place the treat on the floor, but be ready to cover it quickly. While sitting in front of your dog, place a treat on the floor close to you but about two feet away from your dog and say "Leave It" in a firm, clear voice. If your dog springs for the treat, say "Uh-oh!" and cover the treat with your hand. Don't push your dog back or pull them away from it.

STEP 6

Repeat Step 5. If your dog leaves the treat on the floor, jackpot them with high-value treats! Over time, keep placing treats on the floor, moving them closer and closer to your dog, and rewarding them—until you can place one directly between their two front paws.

STEP 7

Increase the difficulty by adding movement. Sit in front of your dog and toss a low-value treat away from them. Say "Leave It" before the treat lands on the floor. If your pup lunges for the treat, cover it with your hand.

STEP 8

You can also practice "Leave It" along with "Wait" when feeding your dog's meals or while on walks. City dogs will need a lot of practice with "Leave It" while on walks (since there are all kinds of tempting, stinky things on city sidewalks), so you'll want to leave extra time when they are first learning it. Make sure to bring plenty of very high-value treats that are even more interesting than the "street snacks."

SAFETY

If you need help covering treats on the floor quickly enough, ask an adult to join you. Make sure everyone is calm when moving to cover up the treats. If you get overexcited, your dog may think you are playing a game and they'll try even harder to get the treats on the floor instead of learning to ignore them.

TIPS

PROBLEM SOLVING

When teaching "Leave It," your dog needs to learn to leave treats on the floor alone, even after the exercise is finished. Don't let your dog "help you" clean up by eating the snacks off the floor. The goal is to teach your dog to not eat anything off the floor, even if it is their treat. If your dog tries to eat these snacks, remove the snacks and distract them with a toy or different activity.

PUPPY

You can practice "Leave It" with any object your puppy wants to chew on. Try practicing "Leave It" with furniture, curtains, shoes—whatever! 🐾

④

CLEVER TRICKS

Clever tricks are also known as "fashion commands." These are commands that dogs do not need to know, but are fun ways to show off their skills. Teaching your dog fun tricks keeps their mind busy, and dogs love to learn! Your dog can learn clever tricks once they have a good knowledge of basic commands.

"TAKE IT"

Before you play fetch with your dog, you'll want to teach your pup the basics of the game. This starts with "Take It"! "Take It" will help your dog get comfortable holding a toy in their mouth for a longer time.

ITEMS NEEDED

▷ **A bag or pouch of low-value treats**

▷ **A small container of high-value treats**

▷ **A low-value toy to start**

STEP 1

Sit or kneel on the floor with your dog. Place one of their low-value toys on the floor near you. As soon as your dog touches their toy with their mouth, reward them with your marker word and a low-value treat. Pick up the toy and put it back down. Repeat this step five times.

STEP 2

The goal is to have your dog pick up the toy and hold it in their mouth. Start to only mark and reward your dog when they pick up their toy. After five successful times, start to increase the amount of time they hold the toy in their mouth before getting a treat. The longer they can hold the toy, the more treats they should get.

STEP 3

When your dog is comfortable picking up a toy from the floor and holding it in their mouth for up to 15 seconds, you can teach them to take the toy from out of your hand. Repeat Steps 1 and 2, as you slowly teach your dog that you are inviting them to take something out of your hand.

STEP 4

Once your dog picks up the toy from your hand 10 times in a row successfully, add the verbal command "Take It," by saying the command before they move to take the toy.

STEP 5

Switch out the low-value toy for a high-value toy, as well as different safe objects that they can pick up and hold in their mouth. Only train your dog to pick up objects that are not too heavy for their size and not too confusing to pick up (i.e., a box, a pen, or anything that can be too large or smooth a surface to grip with their mouths, or too small and can be easily swallowed).

TIPS

PROBLEM SOLVING

Your dog may be limited on the size of items they can hold with their mouth, or they may have a hard time holding an object for longer than two seconds. Stick to what they can do for up to a week before adding another challenge. Use high-value toys for dogs who need extra encouragement. 🐾

SAFETY

Teaching "Take It" is the same kind of lesson as "Leave It" and "Drop It." If your dog does resource guarding (page 65) and doesn't want to let go of the toy, you can offer a trade for something equally valuable. Be patient and don't force an object into your dog's mouth. Just like forcefully removing an object, forcing an object into your dog's mouth will confuse and scare them. It will also send the wrong message about how they are supposed to pick up objects from your hand. Just think, if your dog learns to take objects forcefully from your hand, they may do the same with a younger child or someone who is just learning to be comfortable with dogs.

"LEAP"

Your dog will learn how to leap over a stick, a hula hoop, or another object!

ITEMS NEEDED

- ▷ **A small container of high-value treats**
- ▷ **A large room or a yard with space**
- ▷ **A stick or dowel**
- ▷ **2 blocks of wood (stacked books work well, too)**

STEP 1

Set up an area to teach your dog to "Leap" and make sure there's enough space to be safe. To start, put the stick or dowel on the ground. With your dog calmly sitting or standing on one side of the stick and you standing on the other side, place a small piece of high-value treat in one fist. Hold out your fist to let your dog sniff without moving. Now pull your hand downward to the stick so the dog follows your fist. This will help your dog understand that the stick is part of the game.

STEP 2

Bring your extended arm and fist eye level with your dog. Now, pull your fist toward you and allow your dog to walk over the stick to follow. Reward them with a treat. Repeat this exercise five times.

STEP 3

Now raise the stick a few inches by placing each end on a block of wood or a small stack of books. Repeat Step 2, but this time, say "Leap" each time your dog walks or jumps over the stick. It may still be low enough for them to step over, and that's okay! When they complete the "Leap," offer them praise and a treat. Repeat this exercise 5 to 10 times.

STEP 4

When your dog gets the hang of this trick, you can raise the stick a little higher, but always keep it at a safe level for your dog. Once they're an expert at the "Leap" command, you can make the game more fun. Try swapping out the stick with another item, even a hula hoop!

TIPS

PROBLEM SOLVING

If your dog tries to walk around the stick instead of jumping over it, guide them back to the starting position. Lower the stick back to the ground and practice Steps 1 and 2 a few more times before raising it again. 🐾

SAFETY

Never ask a dog to jump higher or longer than they are able to. Remember that younger dogs are able to play games for longer than older dogs. Also, some dogs are physically better at leaping, while others can't jump more than a few inches off the ground. Always pay attention to your dog's limitations and don't push too hard.

"CRAWL"

Your dog will learn how to crawl across the carpet or the grass!

ITEMS NEEDED

▷ **A small container of high-value treats**

▷ **A carpeted room or grassy yard**

Learn this first: "Down"
(page 60)

STEP 1

Start by asking your dog to lie "Down" in a room with plenty of floor space. A room with a carpet or grassy yard is best so your pup's elbows won't get sore as they move forward in a crouch.

STEP 2

Place high-value treats in one fist and allow your dog to sniff them. Once they know there's a reward involved, slowly pull your hand forward along the floor, away from your dog's nose, so they inch forward. If they move forward in a crawl without rising, reward them with praise and a treat. If your dog rises to follow your hand, stop and have them lie down again without giving them the treat. It may take a few tries for your dog to understand that they can move forward without getting up. Repeat this activity five times.

STEP 3

Once your dog knows what you want them to do, repeat the exercise. But this time, say the command "Crawl" each time you pull your fist with the treat along the floor. Repeat this as many times as needed until your dog connects the "Crawl" command with the activity.

STEP 4

Step back a few feet from your dog, and say the command "Crawl" again, without dragging the treat on the ground. If your dog crawls forward without standing up, praise them and give them a treat. Repeat this five times. If your dog stands to come to you, try beginning at Step 3 once again.

TIPS

PROBLEM SOLVING

If your dog repeatedly stands after lying down, they may need to practice the "Down" command. Also, if you only have your dog move forward an inch or two at a time, this might help your dog focus on staying down to move instead of bouncing up with excitement. You can increase their crawl from a few inches to a few feet over a few days of practice, but moving too fast can frustrate you and your pup. It's best to just take your time.

SAFETY

- Don't ask your pup to crawl on hard surfaces. That can be difficult and painful on their elbows.

- If your dog is older, crawling may not be something they can do comfortably. Always pay attention to your dog's limitations and don't ask them to do a trick that seems uncomfortable.

"TUNNEL"

Your dog will learn how to go through a tunnel—your legs!

ITEMS NEEDED

▷ A small container of high-value treats

▷ Your own two legs!

Learn this first: "Sit" (page 52) and "Stay" (page 74). Also learn "Crawl" (page 86) if you have a big dog.

STEP 1

Begin by asking your dog to "Sit" and "Stay." Place a high-value treat in one fist and allow your dog to sniff it.

STEP 2

Facing your dog, stand in front of them with your legs wide apart, like you're sitting on a horse.

STEP 3

Hold your fist with the treat behind you and between your legs so your dog sees it. You may have to twist a little! Tell your dog "Tunnel" as they move forward toward the treat. Move your treat hand back and away so your dog has to move through your legs completely. If they walk through your legs, praise and reward them with the treat. If they hesitate and don't want to walk under you, start again from Step 1. Repeat this exercise until your dog connects the word "Tunnel" with the action of walking between your legs.

STEP 4

Once your dog understands the "Tunnel" command, you can impress friends and family by jumping into position without warning and shouting "Tunnel!" to your dog, who will be thrilled to show off their new skills.

TIPS

PROBLEM SOLVING

- Some dogs are hesitant about moving under things (or people, in this case). It may take these dogs a little longer to learn this trick, but if you're patient and keep trying, any dog should be able to master the tunnel.

- Small dogs will have an easier time with this trick than large dogs because they have an easier time fitting through the tunnel, but large dogs can still learn—especially if they already know the "Crawl" command! 🐾

SAFETY

Don't practice this trick on a hard floor. If your dog knocks you over while going between your legs, you'll want to fall on something soft! A carpeted room or a grassy yard are great places to practice this trick without getting hurt.

"GET EXCITED!"

Your dog will learn how to show their excitement with a happy dance!

ITEMS NEEDED

▷ **A small container of high-value treats**

Learn this first: "Sit" *(page 52) and* "Place" *(page 69)*

STEP 1

Start with your dog in a standing position in front of you. Place a small high-value treat in your fist. Hold out your treat fist to your dog and allow them to sniff.

STEP 2

Use the treat fist to lure your dog to walk in a circle at medium speed. Keep your treat fist in front of their nose so they follow. When they complete a full circle, give them the treat. Repeat five times.

STEP 3

Now, raise your treat fist to just above your dog's head and make a large circle with your fist. Your dog should still follow, with a little bounce in their step as they will try to reach the treat. Have them make two full circles before marking and giving them a treat. Repeat this lesson four more times.

STEP 4

Now, hold your arm out without a treat in your hand. Make a big circle just above the height of your dog with your open hand, and say "Get Excited!" Use an excited voice to encourage their bounciness! Only treat them when they bounce around in two full circles.

TIPS

If your dog does "Get Excited" without being asked to, do not reward their behavior with treats or attention. Redirect their energy into another command, such as "Sit" or "Place" and reward them for that instead. 🐾

SAFETY

Don't hold your treat fist too high above your dog's head. This will tempt your pup to jump up and get the treat with their mouth. If your dog is jumping up and down while moving in a circle, lower the treat a bit.

"REST"

Your dog will learn how to rest their chin on your lap.

ITEMS NEEDED

▷ **A small container of high-value treats**

Learn this first: "Down" (page 60)

STEP 1

Chin resting is a polite way for a dog to greet someone who is seated, when your dog is called over to them. Begin by sitting on the floor with your legs straight out in front of you. Call your dog over and ask them to do "Down" next to you.

STEP 2

Have a treat in the hand opposite from the side your dog is lying on. Make a fist around the treat, reach across your lap, and let your dog have a sniff of your fist.

STEP 3

Once you have your dog's attention, slowly bring your fist from their nose, back onto your lap to lure them, and then across your lap just far enough that your dog's chin rests on your leg. Don't move too quickly, or your dog might jump up from their "Down" position so they can follow your treat hand.

STEP 4

When your dog lays their head on your lap, wait for two seconds before marking, treating, and praising them. Repeat this successfully 10 times in a row before adding in the verbal command "Rest."

STEP 5

Repeat the trick, wait two seconds, and then say the command "Rest." Wait one more second, then reward your dog with the marker word and a treat.

STEP 6

Continue to practice with the hand motions and the verbal command for another week or so. Then start to ask for the command without the hand motions. You can even pat your leg and follow that motion with the verbal command "Rest." Only reward your dog when they rest their chin on your lap and stay there for at least a few seconds.

If your dog is large enough, you can even teach them to do "Rest" on command while you are seated in a chair, on a couch, or on your bed.

TIPS

PROBLEM SOLVING

It's important to be patient with your dog while they are learning this trick. When first learning, they may pop their head up the second you mark their behavior. Calmly start over and see how many times in a row your dog can successfully do "Rest." See if they can consistently do it twice in a row, five times in a row, and so on. Slowly increase the amount of time they hold the "Rest" position, and don't forget to reward them! 🐾

SAFETY

If your dog is very motivated by food, they may climb on top of you to get the treat you are luring them with. If this happens, use lower-value treats so they still have fun without getting too excited.

"BOW"

Your dog will learn how to bow as an introduction to playtime.

ITEMS NEEDED

▷ A small container of high-value treats

STEP 1

When dogs invite each other to play, they bow, stretching out their front paws and raising their hind end. You can practice a dog's bow in the same way. Put yourself in front of your dog in a kneeling position. Bow playfully and quickly, throw your arms down in front of you so you're leaning on your elbows, and stick your rear end in the air. By doing this action, you're inviting your dog to play with you. If they bow back at you, instantly reward them with praise and a treat. Repeat this several times.

STEP 2

After your dog begins to respond to your bow position, you can add the voice command "Bow" when you get in this position. When your dog returns a play bow, reward them with praise and a treat. Repeat this several times.

STEP 3

Over time, you should be able to give the "Bow" command without having to bow yourself, and your dog will perform it when you ask.

SAFETY

Don't get too close to your dog when you're down on all fours. Make sure you've left enough personal space so your dog doesn't feel threatened by you and your actions.

TIPS

PROBLEM SOLVING

Some dogs, especially older dogs, may not pick up the "Bow" command quickly. One way to teach this trick is to catch your dog in a stretch, then say the word "Bow" when you see them stretching downward. Immediately praise them and give them a treat. This method might take longer, but over time, it can help an older dog understand what you're asking them to do. 🐾

"PAW"

Your dog will learn how to give you their paw to hold in their very own handshake.

> ### ITEMS NEEDED
>
> ▷ **A small container of high-value treats**
>
> *Learn this first:* "Sit" *(page 52)*

STEP 1

Take a treat and make a fist around it. Kneel on the floor and ask your dog to come over to you and "Sit."

STEP 2

Move your treat hand toward the side of your dog's muzzle. From there, steadily move your hand downward toward their paw without having their nose follow your hand.

STEP 3

Your dog may try to use their paw to open your treat hand. When their paw touches your hand, mark the behavior with "Nice!" Open your hand and let them have the treat.

STEP 4

Repeat this lesson until your dog lifts their paw when your hand moves downward toward it. When they lift their paw, give them the verbal command "Paw." When their paw touches your hand, give them the reward as you did in Step 3.

STEP 5

When you dog has learned to "Paw" on command with the treat, begin practicing with an open palm and no treat in your hand. Continue to reward them with marker words and lots of praise.

SAFETY

- Be gentle with your dog's paws. They are very sensitive and should not be squeezed. This can startle your dog!

- A dog who learns how to do "Paw" is usually much easier to handle when they need to go to the vet or get their nails cut.

TIPS

PROBLEM SOLVING

If your dog does not lift their paw on their own in Step 3, you can try to gently lift their paw into your hand while you give the command "Paw." If they cooperate, reward them with the marker word and treats.

PUPPY

"Shake" or "Paw" is great to teach a puppy because it will help them adjust to being handled by a vet or groomer.

"BRING IT"

Your dog will learn how to pick up an item and bring it to you!

ITEMS NEEDED

- ▷ **A bag or pouch of low-value treats**
- ▷ **A dog toy or object that is easy for your dog to pick up and hold in their mouth**
- ▷ **Another human to assist**

Learn this first: "Take It" (page 82) and "Drop It" (page 63). The dog should also know their name.

STEP 1

Start by sitting in front of your dog, with your human assistant sitting four feet across from you. Your assistant should have some treats in their pocket, ready to reward your pup.

STEP 2

With your dog's toy or other object in your hands, give your dog the "Take It" command. Have them hold the object in their mouth for a few seconds, but do not reward them.

STEP 3

Have your assistant call your dog over to them by saying the dog's name, taking a slight pause, then saying "Bring it!" The assistant should hold both hands out in front of them with palms up, ready for your dog to drop the toy into their hands. Have your assistant use a positive, encouraging voice to get your dog to move toward them.

STEP 4

Your dog should keep the toy in their mouth as they walk over to your assistant. As soon as your dog's mouth is over their open hands, they can ask for your dog to "Drop It." It's okay if the toy does not land into their hands just yet. The goal is for your dog to bring and drop their toy from their mouth to give to someone else! If your dog drops the toy close to your assistant, they can still reward your pup with lots of praise and treats.

STEP 5

Repeat Steps 1 through 4. This time, switch roles. Let your assistant give the "Take It" command, and you call your dog over, practicing "Bring It" and "Drop It." Repeat this lesson, taking turns and rewarding the dog, for up to five minutes.

STEP 6

When your dog shows that they're comfortable with this trick, move on to placing the toy on the floor and asking your dog to "Take It," and then "Bring It" to you. Also work on increasing the distance your dog must travel with the object in their mouth.

Eventually, you will be able to do this exercise alone with your dog. Practice with different objects and in different places. This way, your pup can learn to not only pick up unexpected objects when asked, but also to deliver them to you!

TIPS

PROBLEM SOLVING

- When they are first learning, your dog may drop their toy or object when they start walking over to your assistant. If this happens, shorten the distance between you and your assistant. Don't reward your dog with treats if they do not bring the toy close to your assistant. Instead, give them lots of positive talk while they have the toy in their mouth. As your dog moves in the right direction, while keeping the toy in their mouth, cheer them on.

- If your dog gets bored of the toy you are using, try having four toys, two for each human, and make trades with your pup. This will keep them interested because they know they will also be rewarded with the "surprise" of a new toy each time. 🐾

SAFETY

These tricks and commands are meant to build trust between your dog and you. This trick is also designed to reduce the chances of your dog wanting to guard objects, because they know you're a good sharer. If you find that your dog is running away with objects after taking them, don't chase them. Instead, try to use less interesting objects that your pup would be less likely to run off with. Then you can slowly build up toward the toys and objects they treasure.

"HIGH FIVE"

Your cool dog will learn to give you a high five!

ITEMS NEEDED

▷ A small container of high-value treats

Learn this first: "Sit" (page 52) and "Paw" (page 96)

STEP 1

Start with you and your dog sitting in front of each other. Place a treat in your hand and make a fist around it.

STEP 2

Get ready to do "Paw" (page 96) with your treat hand. But as your dog lifts their paw, you will turn your hand so your palm is facing your dog. The goal is to have your dog tap the palm of your hand with their paw.

STEP 3

Repeat this lesson until your pup has mastered doing the "High Five" with your hand right in front of them. Now, hold the palm of your hand out in front of their chest, pause, and say "High Five." When they tap your hand with their paw, mark, treat, and praise them! Repeat successfully five times in a row.

STEP 4

Now try increasing the distance between your dog's chest and your "High Five" hand. This will force your dog to reach out farther with their paw. ▷

TIPS

PROBLEM SOLVING

Your pup might try to "High Five" the palm of your hand with their nose instead of their paw. This is because the "High Five" hand gesture looks like "Touch." Don't reward your pup if they do this—just start over instead. 🐾

SAFETY

• Don't grab hold of your dog's hand when doing "High Five." This will confuse your dog, as that is a completely different trick.

• Dogs get excited, and so your dog may "High Five" very enthusiastically, and accidentally scratch you. If this happens, try wearing a sock over your hand, and only reward your dog when they do "High Five" gently.

"PLAY DEAD"

Your dog will learn how to play dead by dropping down quickly.

ITEMS NEEDED

▷ **A small container of high-value treats**

▷ **A carpeted room or grassy yard**

Learn this first: "Down" (page 60) and "Roll Over" (page 117)

STEP 1

Start in a carpeted room or a grassy yard. Just like in "Roll Over," hold a treat in one fist by the side of your dog's head, right by their muzzle. Slowly and evenly move your treat hand in a curve downward toward the floor, keeping your hand close to your dog's muzzle as they move their head to follow it. The idea is to lure your dog to lie on their side. Once they are on their side and lying calmly, give them praise and a treat. Repeat this exercise five times.

STEP 2

After your dog understands what you're asking them to do, add in the command "Play Dead" and move your hand a little faster in a curve downward to the floor. You want them to connect the words "Play Dead" with moving quickly to the ground. Repeat this step five times.

STEP 3

Repeat the activity without being next to the dog. Try saying "Play Dead" standing a few feet away, then try it standing across the room. With practice, your dog will drop so quickly with this command that they'll be ready for an acting career! ▷

TIPS

PROBLEM SOLVING

If your dog rolls over instead of lying on their side, try slowing down. Excited dogs want to please their human friends, and if your dog already knows how to roll over, they may try to guess (incorrectly) what you're asking them to do. Stay calm and patient and keep trying. It may take a few days to master this trick. 🐾

SAFETY

Never force your dog onto their side. Allow them to roll onto their side naturally. This will help your dog to learn to trust you.

"SPEAK"

Your dog will learn how to bark on command.

ITEMS NEEDED

▷ **A small container of high-value treats**

Learn this first: "Sit" *(page 52)*

STEP 1

Most people don't want their dog to make a lot of noise in the house. After all, dogs can be loud! But here you are simply teaching them how to bark on command. To train your dog to "Speak," place high-value treats in your fist and allow them to sniff it.

STEP 2

Start by asking your dog to "Sit." This will help keep them calm for the activity.

STEP 3

Once your dog is sitting calmly, say their name, followed by the word "Speak." Because your dog won't know what this means yet, you can help them learn by barking at them. Your dog will probably get excited. They might even stand again, and that's okay. The important part is to get your dog to make a noise. Once your pooch makes a noise, even if it's not a full bark, praise and reward them with a treat. Repeat this activity five times.

STEP 4

Once your dog connects noise with the word "Speak," you can be more choosy about giving rewards. Only reward them when they give a full bark after the command. ▷

TIPS

- Your dog may want to stand again or do other tricks when being asked to "Speak." You can gently tell them "Uh-oh" and ask them to sit again before continuing the activity.

- Dogs can get confused learning the "Speak" command, especially if everyone around them has been telling them "Uh-oh" or "No" when they make noise most of the time, but don't be discouraged. Once your dog figures out they're only supposed to speak when asked, it's an easy trick to pick up. 🐾

SAFETY

Don't let your dog get so worked up that they start jumping or pawing. If your dog gets too excited, back off and try the trick again another time.

"FOR SHAME"

Your dog will learn how to look ashamed by rubbing their paw across their nose!

ITEMS NEEDED

▷ **A bag or pouch of low-value treats or kibble**

▷ **Tape or a sticky note**

Learn this first: "Sit" (page 52) or "Down" (page 60)

STEP 1

Begin by asking your dog to "Sit" or lie "Down."

STEP 2

Place a piece of tape or sticky note on your dog's nose. When they paw at it to remove it, praise them and give them a treat. Repeat this exercise 5 to 10 times.

STEP 3

Repeat Step 2, but now say, "For Shame." (To impress friends and family, say this very dramatically.) Each time your dog uses their paw or paws to remove the piece of tape when you say "For Shame," praise them and give them a treat. Repeat this exercise 5 to 10 times if your dog will allow.

STEP 4

Now give your dog the command "For Shame" without putting tape on their nose. When your dog paws their nose, praise them and give them treats.

STEP 5

Work on a routine! Think of times when you could use the words "For Shame" in conversation so you and your dog can perform for others. Here are some ideas:

• "Bella, I can't play. I have too much homework tonight. For shame!"

• "Bella, did you eat that cookie? For shame!"

• "Bella, I heard you chased the cat today. For shame!" ▷

TIPS

PROBLEM SOLVING

Your dog may be distracted by the tape or sticky note, so it may take them some time to connect the words "For Shame" with the action of putting a paw to their nose.

SAFETY

Make sure your dog doesn't eat the tape or sticky note. Take it away when you end your activity.

"WAVE" (HELLO OR GOODBYE)

Everyone will love your friendly dog, because they will know how to wave hello and goodbye!

ITEMS NEEDED

▷ **A small container of low-value treats**

Learn this first: "Paw" (page 96)

STEP 1

Give your dog the command "Paw." When your dog lifts their paw, move your open hand up higher. This will cause your dog to move their paw up higher to reach your hand.

STEP 2

When your dog raises their paw up higher, mark them with "Yes!" or "Nice!" and give them a treat.

STEP 3

Repeat this lesson five more times. Each time, move your hand up a tiny bit higher until your dog is raising their paw alongside their head. When your dog's paw is at the same level as their face, give the verbal command "Wave" and reward them with a treat. Repeat this trick several times and reward them with a treat for each wave.

STEP 4

After your dog gets the hang of this, stop using your hand to lure their hand upward. Just give the command "Wave" and reward them with marker words and lots of praise.

TIPS

PROBLEM SOLVING

"Wave" can be a frustrating trick for dogs to learn—it's hard work! Keep training sessions short and positive. Practice for just a few minutes at a time, once or twice a day. 🐾

"CLEAN UP"

Your dog will learn how to clean up after themselves. Yes, really!

ITEMS NEEDED

▷ **A box or basket to put toys in. Make sure the box is not too tall so your dog can peek their head over the top**

▷ **A few of your dog's favorite toys**

▷ **A bag or pouch of high-value treats**

Learn this first: "Bring It" (page 98), "Drop It" (page 63), "Place" (page 69), and "Touch" (page 50). The dog should also be able to target.

STEP 1

Sit on the floor and place the box near you. Have your dog in the room with you in their "Place."

STEP 2

When you have your dog's attention, calmly toss one of your dog's toys about two feet away from you.

STEP 3

Point to the toy and ask your dog to "Bring It." As your dog walks toward you with the toy in their mouth, point to the box. Don't use a verbal command yet. Allow your dog to walk toward the box with the toy in their mouth.

STEP 4

As they get the toy close to the opening of the box, or has their head over the box, tell your dog to "Drop It." When they release the toy and it falls into the box, reward them with "Yes!" or "Nice!" and a treat.

STEP 5

Repeat Steps 1 to 4 with different toys. As you increase the distance your dog moves with a toy in their mouth to the box, or increase the distance that you sit from the box, reward your dog with more praise and treats!

STEP 6

When your dog has mastered "Clean Up," you can start using this activity for real cleanup! When there are several toys scattered around, place the box nearby and say "Clean Up." Your dog will begin to connect this command with the actions. Reward your pup to keep it fun for them!

TIPS

PROBLEM SOLVING

If your dog seems confused when you point at the box, or moves toward you instead of the box, try placing your hand over the box opening as if you were asking for "Touch." When they touch, you can then say "Drop It." When your dog starts to understand that dropping the toy into the box is what is being rewarded, you can start to point toward the box instead of placing your hand over it. 🐾

"LEAPFROG" (OR "FROGGER")

Your dog will learn how to jump over a person, leapfrog-style!

ITEMS NEEDED

▷ **A small container of high-value treats**

▷ **A large room or a yard with space**

▷ **One or more people**

Learn this first: "Leap" (page 84) and "Stay" (page 74)

STEP 1

Once your dog has mastered the "Leap" command, teaching them "Leapfrog" is easy. It's best to have a few people join in this exercise, but you can also work with just one other person. In a room or a yard with plenty of space, have your person kneel, then tuck their head, arms, and hands inward, pulling their belly close to the ground so their back is flat.

STEP 2

With your dog on one side of your person and you standing on the other side, place a small piece of high-value treat in one fist. Hold out your fist so your dog can sniff.

STEP 3

Ask your dog to "Stay" while you step backward a few feet from your person. You should still be facing your person and your dog. Say "Leap," and pull your fist with the treat back toward you. If your dog is a good leaper, they should understand that you want them to leap over the person on the ground. Practice this exercise several times.

STEP 4

When your dog gets the hang of this trick, have your person rise just a little bit. Practice this, with your person slowly rising a little higher every few times, until they are on their hands and knees with their belly off the ground.

STEP 5

Once your dog is comfortable with leaping over one person, add a second person a few feet away from the first. Make sure there's enough distance between the people for your dog to land the first jump and set up for the second jump. Encourage your dog to "Leap" the second person the same way you had them "Leap" the first. Repeat the exercise, having your dog first jump one person, then the second person, before receiving praise and a treat.

STEP 6

As your dog gets the hang of leapfrogging over more than one person, you can add people until you've got an entire line of friends for them to jump. Just remember to give your pup enough space in between people to land and launch safely! ▶

TIPS

PROBLEM SOLVING

- If you want to make the difference clear between the "Leap" command and the act of leapfrogging, you can teach the word "Frogger" instead. This will help your dog know the difference between jumping one hurdle and jumping multiple people.

- If your dog won't leap over a person, try returning to the "Leap" command using a stick again. A little practice never hurts!

- Little dogs may not be able to jump over a person to land on the other side, but they'll still try, and that may mean landing on your person's back first. Let your people know that this could happen.

- If you're really creative and no one else is around to help, you can try this activity by yourself. Bend down in a doorway and encourage your dog to leapfrog over you to get a treat in the room on the other side. 🐾

SAFETY

- Never ask a dog to jump higher than they are able, and stop if you see them getting tired. To keep your dog safe, always pay attention to their limitations and don't push too hard.

- Let your people know that they might get jumped on in case your dog lands on their back. Have them wear clothing that covers their skin so they don't get scratched.

"PAWS UP"

Your dog will learn how to hold their paws up in front of them as they sit on their hind legs.

ITEMS NEEDED

▷ **A small container of high-value treats**

Learn this first: "Sit" (page 52)

STEP 1

Ask your dog to "Sit." Stand in front of them with both hands behind your back. Each of your hands should have a treat in them.

STEP 2

Put both treat fists in front of their nose and move them both upward at the same time. You are luring your pup to paw both of your hands with their paws, while still sitting. ▶

STEP 3

The moment your dog's front paws both leave the ground, mark the behavior and give them one of the treats.

STEP 4

Repeat this lesson until both of your dog's paws are up by their shoulders; then reward them with the marker word and a treat. When they can keep both paws up for longer than a second, reward them with both treats. Continue to repeat this lesson, each time having your pup hold their paws up for an extra second before giving them treats.

STEP 5

When your dog can hold up their paws for 10 seconds and perform this trick three times in a row, start adding the verbal command "Paws Up!" Move both fists upward and then say "Paws Up!"

TIPS

PROBLEM SOLVING

- You must be quick when you move your treat hands, and quick about marking and rewarding their behavior. You want to reward them when their paws are still up. If you are not quick enough, you may end up rewarding your dog too late, as they're putting their paws back down on the ground.

- Don't move your hands too high up or too quickly. This will cause your dog to move out of their "Sit" position and possibly jump up onto their hind legs. 🐾

"GET BUSY"

Teaching your dog to go potty on command is a great way to keep your yard or neighborhood clean and prevent accidents in areas where dog poop would not be welcomed, like the middle of a sidewalk.

ITEMS NEEDED

▷ **Your dog, leashed up with their walking tools**

▷ **A small container of high-value treats**

STEP 1

Choose a specific spot in your neighborhood or yard where you want them to use the potty.

STEP 2

Whenever it's time to take your dog out to use the bathroom, leash them up and always bring them to this same spot.

STEP 3

Once your dog is at their spot, stay there and let your dog sniff and circle around. Don't let your dog drag you to a different spot.

STEP 4

When your dog starts to pee or poop, say "Get Busy." Wait until they're finished going potty to give them praise and a treat. It may take a few weeks for your pup to connect going potty with the "Get Busy" command.

STEP 5

When your dog starts to connect the "Get Busy" command with the action of going in their busy spot, start saying the "Get Busy" command before they start to relieve themselves. If you say the command and your pup is not relieving themselves, watch their body language. When you notice your dog start to get into position to use the bathroom, say the command "Get Busy." ▶

STEP 6

Once your dog understands that their busy spot and the "Get Busy" command mean that it's time to use the bathroom, start practicing in a different spot. This is so your dog can learn that no matter where they are, they should try to wait until you can find a good place for them to go. When you find that place, you will let them know that it's potty time with their newly learned command.

TIPS

PROBLEM SOLVING

- If your pup begins to relieve themselves before you get to your set busy spot, gently try to put them into a "Sit." Wait for 10 seconds and then continue to the spot and give the "Get Busy" command.

- If this happens a lot when they are first learning the command, try to move the busy spot closer to your home. After they become comfortable with this spot, then you can increase the distance and choose a different busy spot that is farther away. 🐾

SAFETY

Dogs need a regular schedule for potty breaks. Forcing them to hold it for too long in between bathroom breaks can harm their body and make them sick.

"ROLL OVER"

With this trick, you'll teach your dog to roll over.

ITEMS NEEDED

▷ **A favorite blanket or towel**

▷ **A bag or pouch of low-value treats**

Learn this first:
"Sit" (page 52), "Stay" (page 74), and "Down" (page 60)

STEP 1

This trick can be hard to teach because some dogs feel unprotected when they are on their backs. To help your dog feel more comfortable with rolling onto their back, lay their favorite blanket or towel down in front of you.

STEP 2

Ask your dog to "Sit," "Stay," and then "Down" on top of the blanket or towel. Kneel in front of them as they are lying down on top of the blanket.

STEP 3

Hold a treat in your fist by the side of your dog's head, right by their muzzle. Slowly and evenly bring your hand in a curve downward toward the floor, keeping your hand close to your dog's muzzle. The idea is to lure your dog to lie on their side.

STEP 4

Repeat Step 3 from the "Down" position several times, and give your dog treats from your other hand while your dog lies flat on their side with their head on the floor. When your dog can drop down to lie on their side 10 times in a row, you can move on to Step 5.

STEP 5

With your dog lying on their side, continue to move your treat fist in a slow, even motion around your dog's head: from the side, to underneath their chin, over to the other side of their head, and finally to their nose. ▶

Their body should be following along with their head, with your pup ending up lying on their other side. Jackpot treat them when they are able to do this!

STEP 6

Repeat Step 5 until your dog always follows your hand to do the roll-over motion. Then you can start adding in the verbal command "Roll Over" as you move your treat hand to guide your dog.

STEP 7

When your dog can perform this trick with you kneeling in front of them every time, start to increase your distance away from your dog when you give them the command, and perform the hand motion while standing. As your pup gets better at this trick, you can practice without their blanket or towel on a different surface.

TIPS

PROBLEM SOLVING

- "Roll Over" can be one of the most challenging tricks to teach your dog if they have not mastered the basic commands. If they're good at the basics but are still having trouble, make sure that you're not moving your hand too quickly for them to follow along. If your hand moves too quickly, your dog will focus more on playing than on what the movement is trying to teach them.

- Because this is a difficult trick, use different high-value treats to keep your dog engaged.

- For Step 3, if the dog doesn't respond, they may not be aware that there's a treat in your fist. If this is the case, make sure they know there's a treat by opening your fist and showing the treat to them. 🐾

⑤

SUPER FUN
GAMES

Now let's explore some super fun games you and your dog can play together indoors or out that will exercise your bodies and minds. Your dog will need to know basic commands for some of these games, but several can be played no matter what your dog knows!

TUG

ITEMS NEEDED

▷ **A rope or rubber tug toy**

STEP 1

Dogs love a good game of tug-of-war, but it's important to only play this game with the right toys. A thick rope with several knots or a rubber tug toy from a pet store are excellent choices. Get your dog interested in the rope or toy by dangling it in front of them and using an upbeat, excited voice to ask them if they want to play. Allow your dog to grab one end of the toy, but don't let go of your end.

STEP 2

Your dog will put everything they have into tugging and may surprise you with their strength. Let them "win" every now and then by dropping your end of the tug toy. This will help keep them engaged.

TIPS

PROBLEM SOLVING

- Don't play Tug with soft toys like stuffed animals unless you want to clean up a mess of stuffing and replace toys often!

- Some dogs don't like to share their toys and don't understand the game of Tug. They want you to throw the toy. If that's the case, try switching between throwing the rope or tug toy and playing tug-of-war.

- Don't be surprised if your dog growls while playing Tug. Some of the friendliest dogs growl ferociously while tugging on a toy! As long as they are not showing other aggressive behaviors, this is fine. If the dog has forward ears, a wagging tail, and seems relaxed, your dog is playing the right way. Most dog owners begin to know their dogs so well that they can tell the difference between a "play" growl and an "angry" or "fearsome" growl. If you aren't sure, ask a grown-up to help you decide if your dog is having fun.

SAFETY

- Don't drop the tug toy while your dog is actively pulling. Wait until they are only half-pulling. If you let go while your pooch is pulling back, they could fall backward into furniture or walls and hurt themselves.

- For some dogs, tug-of-war is too intense and they can become possessive of the toy. If your dog shows any signs of possessiveness or aggression (page 65), stop playing tug-of-war. Let the dog have the toy, step back, give them a moment to calm down, then firmly tell them to "Drop It." Once the dog has dropped the toy, remove it from the room and put it in a place where they can no longer see it.

TREASURE HUNT

ITEMS NEEDED

▷ High-value or low-value treats, depending on the dog's experience with the game

▷ Hiding places

STEP 1

Treasure Hunt is another kind of hide-and-seek—this one encourages your dog to use their nose. Start by putting your dog in a closed room where you won't be hiding treats. (If they see you walking around with treats in your hand, you'll never get a chance to hide them!)

STEP 2

Once your dog is behind a closed door, hide high-value treats like small pieces of cheese around the house for your dog. Make the hiding spots super easy. For example, place a treat in the upstairs hall, on the floor by the kitchen sink, under the dining room table, etc.

STEP 3

After you've finished hiding all the treats, open the door and let your dog out.

STEP 4

Since your dog won't know how the game is played, you may have to help them figure it out. In an excited voice, say your dog's name followed by "Treasure Hunt!" Your pup will probably get excited, though they won't yet know why.

STEP 5

Help them locate the treats throughout the house. Your dog will get to know the game and look forward to playing. (And you probably won't have to keep pointing out the hiding spots!) After the first few games, you can switch to using low-value treats or pieces of kibble. It will still be just as exciting for your dog and healthier in the long run.

TIPS

PROBLEM SOLVING

You might have to show your dog each hiding spot in the beginning until your dog understands what this game is all about. Be patient. Once your dog learns to use their nose, they'll be on the hunt for those treats as soon as you release them from their waiting spot! 🐾

SAFETY

Don't put treats anywhere unsafe for your dog to lick, such as under a toilet or in a dusty corner. If you play this game outside, watch where your dog goes and make sure they aren't eating anything they shouldn't be, like mushrooms or bugs!

MIX-UP CUPS

ITEMS NEEDED

▷ 3 large plastic drinking cups

▷ A tennis ball

▷ Enough space for fetch

Learn this first: Fetch (page 133), "Drop It" (page 63) "Sit" (page 52), and "Down" (page 60)

STEP 1

If your dog already knows the game of Fetch, you can put a spin on it by introducing them to Mix-Up Cups. Start by having your dog "Sit" or lie "Down." Place three upside-down cups next to each other on the floor in front of your dog.

STEP 2

While your dog is watching, put a tennis ball (or any small dog toy) inside one of the cups, then cover it again.

STEP 3

With your dog watching, move the cups around. You can switch them so the one on the right is in the middle, then the one on the left is in the middle, then the two on the ends are switched. Choose any combination you'd like. There are no rules!

STEP 4

Stop moving the cups and see if your dog can find the ball. Ask them "Where's the ball?" in an excited voice. Your dog might then nudge a cup with their nose or paw at it.

STEP 5

If your dog guesses the correct cup, show them the ball and throw it as a reward. When your dog fetches the ball and brings it back to you, have them "Drop It" and play another round of Mix-Up Cups.

TIPS

PROBLEM SOLVING

Some dogs don't understand this game right away, and some dogs don't care for tennis balls. If your dog prefers, you can use a high-value treat instead of the tennis ball, and your dog will be much more interested in picking the right cup.

SAFETY

When you're done playing the game, make sure to put the cups away. Other-wise, your dog might decide to chew on them since they were part of a game.

RUNAWAY HOSE

ITEMS NEEDED

▷ An outdoor garden hose hooked to a faucet

▷ A hot day

STEP 1

Do this activity in an enclosed outdoor space. Start by bringing your unleashed dog into the yard with you.

STEP 2

Grab the hose and let your dog sniff it before turning it on.

STEP 3

Turn the water on slowly so your dog sees the water as it begins to flow from the hose.

STEP 4

Now comes the fun part! Pick up the hose and aim the water upward, away from your dog. Encourage them to chase the water stream.

STEP 5

At this point, your dog may try to catch the water in their mouth. Wave the hose and send the water streaming in different directions to keep your dog guessing where it will be next.

STEP 6

Dry your dog off with a towel and the sun before going inside.

TIPS

GOOD TO KNOW

While most dogs love water, no one likes a cold bath in the winter, so save this game for a hot summer day.

PROBLEM SOLVING

You'll want to introduce your dog to the hose slowly or they might be afraid of it forever! Be sure to move through these steps at a speed your dog can handle.

SAFETY

- Never spray a dog directly in the face. Your dog will develop a fear of water and the hose, and will begin to mistrust you.

- Never hold your dog on a leash while spraying them with water. They will feel trapped and think that you can't be trusted.

- Not all dogs love water or playing with the hose. If your dog shows signs of fear or agitation, like cowering, tucking their tail between their legs, or laying their ears against the back of their head, stop playing the game. Your dog isn't having as much fun as you are. Find another game you both enjoy.

- Oh, and only play this game for a short time, or you might end up with a mud pit instead of a backyard!

MUFFIN PAN GAME

ITEMS NEEDED

▷ High-value treats

▷ Muffin pan with 6 or 12 spots

▷ 6 or 12 tennis balls (or small dog toys)

STEP 1

Get an adult's permission to use a muffin pan from the kitchen before setting up this game.

STEP 2

Before your dog sees the game, place two to four small pieces of treats in a few different holes in the muffin pan, leaving most of the spots empty. Then cover all of the holes with tennis balls so your dog can't see what's under them. (Small dog toys work well, too, as long as they cover the holes completely.)

STEP 3

When the game is all set up, place the muffin pan on the floor where you want your dog to play the game and call them over.

STEP 4

Watch your pooch figure out which of the muffin holes have treats and which don't!

STEP 5

Repeat the game as many times as you want, as long as your dog is still interested.

STEP 6

Wash the muffin pan with warm, soapy water before returning it to a kitchen cabinet. (Your grown-ups will be impressed!)

SAFETY

Wash the muffin pan thoroughly with warm, soapy water before returning it to the kitchen cabinet. Dogs and people both carry germs, but we carry different kinds and sharing your dog's germs can possibly make you sick. Besides, you wouldn't want to eat a muffin made in a pan your dog just slobbered on, right?

TIPS

PROBLEM SOLVING

- If your dog doesn't understand the game at first, encourage them by picking up one of the balls to show them the treat underneath. You can also tap the ball and say "What's this? Is this your ball?" in an excited voice.

- After your dog gets the hang of this game, you can replace high-value treats with low-value treats or kibble, but you'll want something that smells really good for the first few tries.

- Some dogs get SO excited to see tennis balls that they may not even care about the treats inside the muffin tin. That's perfectly okay! As long as your dog enjoys the game, we won't judge how they play. 🐾

BUBBLE CATCH

ITEMS NEEDED

▷ Bubble solution and bubble wand

STEP 1

Dogs are a lot like human toddlers, and many of them are amazed by bubbles. Blow just one or two to start, and encourage your dog to chase them. Point them out and watch as your dog tracks the bubbles with their eyes.

STEP 2

Catch a bubble in your hand and let your dog sniff and pop it. Before long, your dog will be snatching bubbles out of the air and popping them by themselves!

TIPS

PROBLEM SOLVING

Don't blow too many bubbles right away. Your dog may get overwhelmed and not know what to do! Start with just a few bubbles. After your dog gets the hang of chasing them, you can start to blow more.

SAFETY

- Avoid blowing bubbles directly in a dog's face.

- Limit this game to a few minutes at a time. Your dog is using their mouth to pop the bubbles, and while it's harmless, you don't want your dog to eat too much solution.

- Offer lots of water afterward so your dog can wash out the taste of bubbles.

- This is a great outdoor game. Ask your grown-up first before playing inside. If you play indoors, make sure you clean the floor afterward with a towel. Bubbles can make things slippery!

FETCH

ITEMS NEEDED

▷ **A favorite ball or toy**

Learn this first: "Drop It" (page 63) and "Sit" (page 52)

STEP 1

Most dogs are natural runners and retrievers. They are born to chase! The game of Fetch works with this natural urge, and it can be played indoors or out. If you play it indoors, find an open space away from any fragile items, like the TV, glass items, or computer.

STEP 2

Pick one of your dog's favorite toys—one that's good for throwing. If playing indoors, a soft toy works great. If playing outdoors, try a tennis ball or other rubber dog ball.

STEP 3

Next, get your dog's attention by calling their name or waving the toy in the air.

STEP 4

Ask your dog to "Sit," then toss the toy across the room or yard and watch your dog race to get it.

STEP 5

When your dog grabs the toy, call them back again. Use the "Drop It" command so they drop the toy and you can throw it again.

TIPS

PROBLEM SOLVING

It takes some dogs a while to understand they're supposed to return to you with the toy. Some dogs are just so happy to have their toy, they'll prance around the house or yard with it in their mouth. Be patient, and keep calling your dog until they return.

SAFETY

• Don't try to grab a toy from your dog's mouth if they aren't letting go. Wait for them to drop it, so you don't accidentally get bitten.

• If playing indoors, don't throw the toy too hard: a gentle toss will do!

FRISBEE

ITEMS NEEDED

▷ **A frisbee**

▷ **An outdoor space**

Learn this first: "Drop It" (page 63) and "Sit" (page 52)

STEP 1

Take Fetch up a notch and teach your dog to catch a frisbee! Unlike Fetch, this is an outdoor-only kind of game. Pick your outdoor spot.

STEP 2

Ask your dog to "Sit," and hold the frisbee out for them to see. Don't let them take it just yet.

STEP 3

Once your dog has seen the frisbee, toss it gently and not too far. Most dogs won't catch it the first few times. A frisbee flies differently through the air than a ball and it may take your dog a while to figure out how to grab it.

STEP 4

Even if your dog doesn't catch the frisbee, they can still fetch it and bring it back to you. Ask them to "Drop It," and offer lots of praise for the returned frisbee.

STEP 5

As your dog begins to learn the way a frisbee flies and how to catch it, you can increase the distance you throw it.

TIPS

PROBLEM SOLVING

Some dogs are natural frisbee champions (such as herding dogs), but not all dogs have the instincts to jump and catch a frisbee in midair. If your dog seems interested in retrieving it, but not in catching it, perhaps the game of fetch is more their speed.

SAFETY

Don't throw a frisbee farther than your dog can run (like outside a fenced area), or into obstacles like bushes or rocks. Your dog will be watching the frisbee as it flies through the air and they may not see obstacles that could hurt them.

SOCCER

ITEMS NEEDED

▷ A small container of high-value treats

▷ A soccer ball (or other kick ball)

STEP 1

Believe it or not, this game starts indoors! Place the ball on the floor and let the dog sniff it. When they sniff the ball, they will likely accidentally move it in some way. Praise them and give them a treat.

STEP 2

Each time your dog touches the ball, give them praise and a treat. Repeat a few times until your dog figures out that touching the ball gets them a treat.

STEP 3

Sit on the floor near your dog. Point out the ball by moving it with your hands back and forth on the floor. Then roll it to your dog. If your dog changes the direction of the ball's roll with either a nose or a paw, praise them and offer them a treat. Repeat this five times.

STEP 4

Bring the game outside. Continue repeating Step 3 in your yard, but this time do it while standing. You can even increase the distance between you and your dog.

STEP 5

Now, instead of rolling the ball to your dog with your hands, begin to gently kick it with your feet, and see if you can get your dog to join in. ▶

STEP 6

The more you play, the better your dog will get. When the two of you have gotten really good at playing soccer together, your dog will know where you're going to kick the ball and will probably be there to meet the ball and send it back to you!

TIPS

GOOD TO KNOW

Some breeds are better suited to playing soccer than others—especially high-energy herding dogs—but you can try to teach your dog to play soccer no matter what breed they are.

PROBLEM SOLVING

Try playing soccer with a smaller or larger ball, depending on your dog's breed and size. Smaller dogs can still move a soccer ball around, but they might have an easier time with a smaller, lighter ball. 🐾

SAFETY

Don't kick the ball directly to your dog with force. Your dog doesn't have goalie gear and can't protect themselves from the impact.

ROLL IT

ITEMS NEEDED

- ▷ **A plastic tennis ball container with lid OR empty plastic soft drink bottle with cap**
- ▷ **Low-value treats**
- ▷ **A marker**
- ▷ **Scissors or utility knife**
- ▷ **Adult supervision/ help**

STEP 1

For this game, you'll create a container your dog can roll around the floor with their nose in order to receive treats. Use the marker to mark two or three places on the outside of the tennis ball container or soft drink bottle you want to cut small holes into. On different sides of the bottle, mark one hole toward the top of the container, one hole toward the bottom, and one somewhere in the middle. Don't put them all on the same side.

The holes should be just a little bit bigger than the size of the treats you'll be placing inside. If the holes are too big, your dog will knock all the treats out right away. If they are too small, your dog will get frustrated that they can't get the treats at all.

STEP 2

Have an adult help you cut the holes into the plastic. Make sure there are no sharp edges along the holes.

STEP 3

Place 5 to 10 pieces of low-value treats into the container and make sure the lid is tightly sealed. Test the toy by rolling it straight across the floor. Your toy should dispense a few treats here and there as it rolls.

STEP 4

Introduce the toy to your dog. Give it a few shakes so your dog gets excited about it, then place it on the floor and watch them figure out just how to move it. ▶

They'll soon learn that spinning it won't dispense treats—only rolling will! A patient dog will figure out how to nose the toy across the floor to get what they want.

TIPS

PROBLEM SOLVING

- If the treats dispense too quickly, you may have made your holes too big. Cover those with paper and try again with smaller holes.

- If the treats won't come out, try making the holes larger or adding a few more holes to the toy.

- This is a great way to feed dogs who wolf down their food too quickly! Putting kibble into the container and letting them roll it around the floor will help slow them down at mealtime.

HIDE-AND-SEEK

ITEMS NEEDED

▷ Just you and your dog

▷ Another person to help for the first few games (optional)

Learn this first: "Sit" (*page 52*) *and* "Stay" (*page 74*)

STEP 1

Playing Hide-and-Seek with your dog is tons of fun, but you'll probably have to do all the hiding! This game can be played indoors or out—anywhere you can find enough hiding spots.

STEP 2

Choose a place to ask your dog to "Sit" and "Stay." This place should be used every time you play the game, so your dog learns what they need to do when asked to sit and stay in that exact spot.

STEP 3

Walk away from your dog and find a hiding place in another part of your house. If your dog jumps up the moment you're out of sight, you may need to have a helper keep them in place with the "Stay" command while you leave the room.

STEP 4

Once you've found your hiding spot, call your dog to find you. If your dog likes to use their nose, you may only have to call once before they "seek you out." If your dog is new to the game, you may need to keep calling them to come find you. ▶

STEP 5

When your dog finds you, get excited about it! Give them lots of praise and pets. Then, return your dog to the same sitting area you used in Step 2 and play again. With practice, your dog will learn that sitting and staying is part of the game, and they won't move until you call them.

TIPS

PROBLEM SOLVING

Some dogs will grow tired of "seeking" or may become distracted. If this happens, keep calling your dog so they don't forget they're supposed to be looking for you! 🐾

SAFETY

Don't hide anywhere too small for you or anywhere you can't escape from on your own. Never hide in appliances like dishwashers, refrigerators, or freezers. And always keep your hiding spots easy to find. After all, you're playing with a dog, not a human!

FLIP IT

ITEMS NEEDED

▷ 3 or 4 empty plastic soft drink bottles without caps

▷ Low-value treats

▷ A marker

▷ Scissors or utility knife

▷ A stick or dowel 3 feet in length

▷ 2 kitchen chairs (or outdoor chairs if playing outside)

▷ Adult supervision

STEP 1

Just like Roll It, Flip It requires you to adjust a few containers so your dog can play in order to receive their treats. This time, you'll leave the bottles whole (no treat holes), but you'll still need to cut two holes near the neck (top) of the bottles to place them on your stick or dowel. Using your marker, mark two spots on each container where you'll cut holes to slide your stick straight through the neck of the bottle.

STEP 2

Have an adult help you cut into the plastic, until the holes are completely cut out. Make sure there are no sharp edges along the holes. Repeat for each container.

STEP 3

Place your stick or dowel through the holes in all of your containers. Then hold one end of the stick in each hand. Your containers should rest with their bottoms facing down and the opening of the bottles facing up. Try swinging them back and forth to make sure they move freely and can be flipped upside down and back again easily. If they get stuck, you might need to widen the holes.

STEP 4

Once the bottles flip easily, take your stick (loaded with your bottles) and place it between the seats of two chairs to hold it up a few feet off the floor. Make sure it's secure, because your dog will paw at the bottles and might knock the whole thing down if the stick isn't secure.

STEP 5

Place a few pieces of low-value treat or kibble in each of the containers and introduce your dog to the game. Watch as they figure out the trick: The bottles need to be flipped upside down in order to dispense the treats!

TIPS

PROBLEM SOLVING

If your dog gets frustrated, help them by tipping the bottles to dispense the treats. Some dogs don't understand how the bottles need to move, but if you play this game often, your dog will start flipping the bottles before you've even filled them with treats! 🐾

FIND IT

ITEMS NEEDED

▷ **A bag or pouch of low-value treats**

▷ **Your dog's favorite toy**

STEP 1

Find It is a great game to play with your dog's favorite toy. Played indoors or out, this game is a sneakier version of the "Bring It" trick. Start by showing your dog their favorite toy and getting them excited.

STEP 2

While your dog isn't looking, hide the toy somewhere in the house or yard for them to find. If you need to, you can have your dog wait in another room behind a closed door.

STEP 3

Let your dog out of the room and ask them to bring you the toy you hid. Your dog may go to all the usual spots they keep their toy and be puzzled when it's not there.

STEP 4

Make a show of looking around the house with them, and keep asking them to bring you the toy.

STEP 5

Lead your dog to the place where you've hidden the toy, but don't point it out right away. See if your dog can find it on their own.

STEP 6

When they find the toy, reward them with praise and treats. Play this game as many times as you'd like. ▶

TIPS

PROBLEM SOLVING

Your dog may not understand how this game works in the beginning, but after you play it a few times, they will figure out that you've hidden their toy and they need to find it. It's also best if you pick a few "regular" hiding spots so your dog can enjoy the victory of finding the toy on their own. 🐾

SAFETY

Don't hide your dog's toy anywhere they might break furniture or valuables while trying to get to it. Like, no hiding it in glass vases, please! Keep the toy easy to find and easy to get to.

THE NAME GAME

STEP 1

Your dog may already know a bunch of commands and understand the names of several of their toys, but you can teach them the names of many more things. Start by listing the names of items or people you want your dog to know.

STEP 2

Pick one item from your list to teach your dog the first day. Your dog probably won't be able to learn more than that in one sitting, and you don't want to confuse them. For this example, let's say you want your dog to learn who "Mom" is.

STEP 3

Pick a spot in the room for you and your dog to start. You'll return to this spot several times during the exercise. As you stand in your spot, have your mom stand next to you. Say your dog's name, then say "Mom" and point to your mom. Repeat this several times.

STEP 4

Have your mom move 5 to 10 feet away in the same room. Now say your dog's name, then say "Where's Mom?" Then, walk over to your mom and point to her again while saying "Mom." Return to your original spot, and repeat this exercise three times, having your mom move to different places in the room.

STEP 5

Return to your place across the room, asking your dog to come with you. ▶

Then, ask your dog "Where's Mom?" again. If your dog walks to your mom OR looks at your mom, you can reward them with praise and a treat. If they seem confused, walk to your mom again and repeat "Mom" several times. Then try this step once more from the beginning.

STEP 6

Repeat Step 5 as many times as needed until your dog associates the word "Mom" with the person. For the next few weeks, you can make sure your dog doesn't forget the new word by asking them "Where's Mom?" When they find or look at your mom, reward them with praise and a treat.

STEP 7

Have fun with this game, and teach your dog the names of things you'd like them to bring to you (like the newspaper, slippers, the TV remote). Dogs are super smart! You'll be amazed at how many words your dog can learn.

TIPS

PROBLEM SOLVING

- This game is all about repeating. Some dogs pick up the names of items or people very quickly, and other dogs need more time. It may take your dog more than one day to learn the name of one item. Go at the speed that works for your dog.

- Dogs will forget words if they aren't used often. If you want your dog's vocabulary to stay large, play reminder games often and reward them with praise or treats. 🐾

OBSTACLE COURSE

ITEMS NEEDED

▷ Paper and pen

▷ Any or all of the following:

▷ A long stick or dowel

▷ 2 wooden blocks (or a stack of books)

▷ Hula hoop

▷ 2 outdoor chairs

▷ Large cardboard box

▷ Plywood

▷ A large, flat rock

▷ 6 painted sticks (any color) or dowels about 2 feet long

▷ Adult supervision

Learn this first: "Leap" (page 84) and "Tunnel" (page 88)

STEP 1

An obstacle course is a great game to play if your dog already knows tricks like "Leap" and "Tunnel." Design your obstacle course by planning it out on a piece of paper. Draw the shape of your backyard and where you plan to put each obstacle. Space the obstacles wide enough apart so your dog has enough room to move from one obstacle to the next.

STEP 2

You might decide to start your course with a hula hoop, which can either be held by a person or between the backs of two outdoor chairs.

STEP 3

Next, cut open a large cardboard box so it forms a tunnel. Get help if you need it. You can do this either by taking out the bottom of the box or by cutting the entire box open and unfolding it to create a tunnel on the ground. You may want to pin the edges of the box to the ground with heavy rocks or books so it doesn't fly away in a breeze.

STEP 4

Set up your stick or dowel on top of your wooden blocks (or stacks of books) just like you did when you taught your dog the "Leap" command. ▶

STEP 5

Make a ramp for your dog by setting a piece of plywood so one end is in the grass and the other end sits on top of the large, flat rock. Make sure the ramp doesn't wobble by testing it out yourself and jumping off the end. If the ramp seems wobbly, put other rocks underneath or angle it differently until it's safe and secure.

STEP 6

Set up your painted sticks by wedging them straight into the ground one at a time in a straight line anywhere from two to three feet apart, depending on the size of your dog. Bigger dogs will need more space to weave between the sticks.

STEP 7

Introduce your dog to the obstacle course by guiding them through each obstacle one at a time. Use treats to guide them and reward them when they've done what you asked. Hopefully you have already taught them "Tunnel"—if not, you can teach them now (page 88). To teach your pooch to weave through your painted sticks, you'll want to weave through them yourself while holding a treat to lure your dog in and out. You can also take them through the sticks while they're on the leash.

STEP 8

Have fun. If your dog doesn't like any of the obstacles, skip that obstacle and keep going. This is a game—it's meant to be fun! You can even time your dog to see if they can beat their previous record, and reward them when they do! ▶

SAFETY

- Have an adult supervise the setup of your obstacle course. They can cut the box tunnel and help put the heavier pieces (like plywood) in place.
- Make sure the obstacles you create are safe for your dog and that there are no sharp edges or pointy ends that could hurt your dog.

TIPS

PROBLEM SOLVING

- Not every dog will want to do every trick in an obstacle course. Your dog may do one trick naturally, and completely avoid another. For the best success, take your time introducing your dog to each event in the obstacle course.

- The best part about creating your own obstacle course is that you can use any items you have around your home. You can also change the order of obstacles any time. If your dog masters the course or you just get tired of the same order, swap them around and start from scratch. 🐾

PUPPY WALK SCHEDULE & POTTY CHART

(3 TO 6 MONTHS)

DAY OF THE WEEK	MORNING WALK	MID-MORNING WALK	MIDDAY WALK	AFTERNOON WALK	EVENING WALK	NIGHTTIME WALK
MONDAY	6AM	9AM	12PM	3PM	6PM	9PM
PEE	YES NO	YES NO	YES NO	YES NO	YES NO	YES NO
POOP	YES NO	YES NO	YES NO	YES NO	YES NO	YES NO
TUESDAY	6AM	9AM	12PM	3PM	6PM	9PM
PEE	YES NO	YES NO	YES NO	YES NO	YES NO	YES NO
POOP	YES NO	YES NO	YES NO	YES NO	YES NO	YES NO
WEDNESDAY	6AM	9AM	12PM	3PM	6PM	9PM
PEE	YES NO	YES NO	YES NO	YES NO	YES NO	YES NO
POOP	YES NO	YES NO	YES NO	YES NO	YES NO	YES NO
THURSDAY	6AM	9AM	12PM	3PM	6PM	9PM
PEE	YES NO	YES NO	YES NO	YES NO	YES NO	YES NO
POOP	YES NO	YES NO	YES NO	YES NO	YES NO	YES NO
FRIDAY	6AM	9AM	12PM	3PM	6PM	9PM
PEE	YES NO	YES NO	YES NO	YES NO	YES NO	YES NO
POOP	YES NO	YES NO	YES NO	YES NO	YES NO	YES NO
SATURDAY	6AM	9AM	12PM	3PM	6PM	9PM
PEE	YES NO	YES NO	YES NO	YES NO	YES NO	YES NO
POOP	YES NO	YES NO	YES NO	YES NO	YES NO	YES NO
SUNDAY	6AM	9AM	12PM	3PM	6PM	9PM
PEE	YES NO	YES NO	YES NO	YES NO	YES NO	YES NO
POOP	YES NO	YES NO	YES NO	YES NO	YES NO	YES NO

NOTE: During school days, you can skip the Midmorning and Midday Walks.

WALK SCHEDULE & POTTY CHART

(9 MONTHS AND OLDER)

DAY OF THE WEEK	MORNING WALK	MIDDAY WALK	AFTERNOON WALK	NIGHTTIME WALK
MONDAY	TIME:	TIME:	TIME:	TIME:
PEE	YES NO	YES NO	YES NO	YES NO
POOP	YES NO	YES NO	YES NO	YES NO
TUESDAY	TIME:	TIME:	TIME:	TIME:
PEE	YES NO	YES NO	YES NO	YES NO
POOP	YES NO	YES NO	YES NO	YES NO
WEDNESDAY	TIME:	TIME:	TIME:	TIME:
PEE	YES NO	YES NO	YES NO	YES NO
POOP	YES NO	YES NO	YES NO	YES NO
THURSDAY	TIME:	TIME:	TIME:	TIME:
PEE	YES NO	YES NO	YES NO	YES NO
POOP	YES NO	YES NO	YES NO	YES NO
FRIDAY	TIME:	TIME:	TIME:	TIME:
PEE	YES NO	YES NO	YES NO	YES NO
POOP	YES NO	YES NO	YES NO	YES NO
SATURDAY	TIME:	TIME:	TIME:	TIME:
PEE	YES NO	YES NO	YES NO	YES NO
POOP	YES NO	YES NO	YES NO	YES NO
SUNDAY	TIME:	TIME:	TIME:	TIME:
PEE	YES NO	YES NO	YES NO	YES NO
POOP	YES NO	YES NO	YES NO	YES NO

NOTE: Write in what time you went for the walk. You can skip Midday Walks during school, but it's best not to make a dog wait longer than 8 hours in between potty breaks.

GLOSSARY

BODY LANGUAGE what an animal's body tells us about their emotions

EASY WALK HARNESS a special collar that prevents a dog from pulling away when walking on a leash

GENTLE LEADER a head collar that helps control a dog and prevent them from pulling when walking on a leash

HEAD HALTER a head accessory that helps control a dog when walking them on a leash

HIGH-VALUE TREAT a treat of greater interest, such as cooked chicken or peanut butter

HOUSEBROKEN potty trained

JACKPOT a reward of several treats at once

KIBBLE dry dog food

LONG LEAD a long dog run or leash that allows the dog to roam more freely

LOW VALUE TREAT a treat such as dry dog food or small biscuit

LURE to encourage or beckon

MARKER WORD a short word of praise for a good behavior (such as "Yes" or "Good")

MARTINGALE COLLAR a special collar that prevents a dog from pulling away when walking on a leash

MUZZLE this can either refer to the area around a dog's nose and mouth, or an accessory that holds the pet's mouth closed for handling

NEUTERED a routine surgery, usually done before a dog is 1 year old, that prevents a male dog from having puppies with a female dog

NOSE TO TOES a method for making a dog lower themselves to the ground

RELEASE WORD a word or sound that signals to your dog that they are done working. It is the tone that is paired with the word that is the major indicator that there has been a shift from work into relaxed mode

RESOURCE GUARDING the act of protecting a wanted item against other animals or people

RETRACTABLE LEASH a springloaded leash that enables the dog or the walker to control their distance from one another

SPAYED a routine surgery, usually done before a dog is 1 year old, that prevents a female dog from having puppies with a male dog

TARGET to aim properly

TREAT HAND the hand that contains the dog's treat

REFERENCES

"6 Healthy Treat Ideas for Dogs." PetMD.com. Accessed August 30, 2019. www.petmd.com /dog/nutrition/6-healthy-treat-ideas-dogs

"Are Onions Poisonous to Dogs?" PetPoison-Helpline.com; Pet Poison Helpline. Accessed July 14, 2019. www.petpoisonhelpline.com /pet-safety-tips/are-onions-poisons-to-dogs

Brutlag, Ahna. **"Chocolate Poisoning in Dogs."** VCAhospitals.com. LifeLearn Inc. 2014. vcahospitals.com/know-your-pet /chocolate-poisoning-in-dogs

Fessenden, Marissa. **"Humans May Have Domesticated Dogs Tens of Thousands of Years Earlier Than Thought."** SmithsonianMag.com. Smithsonian Museum. May 22, 2015. www.smithsonianmag.com/smart-news /humans-may-have-domesticated-dogs-24000-years-earlier-thought-180955374

"Human Foods Dogs Can and Can't Eat." American Kennel Club. Accessed September 4, 2019. www.akc.org/expert-advice/nutrition /human-foods-dogs-can-and-cant-eat

"Introducing Your New Dog to Other Dogs." The Humane Society of the United States. Accessed August 31, 2019. www.humanesociety.org /resources/introducing-new-dogs

Ollila, Erin. **"Interpreting Common Dog Behaviors & the Meaning Behind His Moods."** HillsPet.com. Hill's Pet Nutrition, Inc. June 13, 2019. www.hillspet.com /dog-care/behavior-appearance /types-of-common-dog-behavior

Reisin, Jan. **"Dog First Aid Kit Essentials."** American Kennel Club. Accessed September 4, 2019. www.akc.org/expert-advice/health /dog-first-aid-kit-essentials

"Teaching Your Dog to Ask to Go Out." WebMD. Accessed August 30, 2019. pets.webmd.com /dogs/guide/teaching-dog-ask-go-out#1

"Training Tip a Guide to Using Food Rewards." AKC Staff. Accessed August 30, 2019. www. akc.org/expert-advice/training /training-tip-food-rewards

"When Dog and Cat Meet." WebMD. Accessed August 31, 2019. pets.webmd.com/features /when-dog-and-cat-meet#1

"Why Do Dogs and Puppies Eat Poop?" PetMd. com. petMD, LLC. Accessed July 14, 2019. www.petmd.com/dog/puppycenter/health /evr_dg_why_do_puppies_eat_poop

Wyant, Liz. **"Top 7 High Value Training Treats."** The Modern Dog Trainer. Accessed August 30, 2019. www.themoderndogtrainer.net /top-7-high-value-training-treats

"Chocolate" https://www.merckvetmanual .com/toxicology/food-hazards/chocolate

"Dog Walking Equipment" http://www.good-dogspot.net/dog-walking-equipment

RESOURCES

- **"FRUITS AND VEGETABLES DOGS CAN OR CAN'T EAT"** www.akc.org/expert-advice/nutrition/ fruits-vegetables-dogs-can-and-cant-eat/
- **"HUMAN FOODS DOGS CAN AND CAN'T EAT"** www.akc.org/expert-advice/nutrition/ human-foods-dogs-can-and-cant-eat/
- **WWW.BEST-DOG-TREAT-RECIPES.COM**
- **DOGTREATKITCHEN.COM**

INDEX

Acknowledgments

I have an enormous amount of gratitude for the team at Penguin Random House for bringing this book into reality—editorial; design; marketing; production; Alisa Harris, the illustrator; my co-writer L. Ryan Storms—but especially my editor Kim Suarez. Kim, your positivity and patience throughout this process have been nothing less than saintly. I am forever grateful to you for this opportunity and for your constant support. If anyone told dog-obsessed childhood me that I would be writing a book for other dog-loving children someday, I would have never believed them. Kim, this is a real thing because of you. Forever, thank you.

My team of superstars at Frolic, and our friends at Biscuits & Bath—I could not have done this without your support. Writing a book and directing after-school programming and summer camps for kids and teens, while caring for dogs, is no easy task. Many thanks to the following people for helping me make Frolic the best place for any dog-loving child: Scott, David, Alexis, Costa, Gabriela, Deannie, JP, Helen.

To my Frolic kids: You inspired everything I wrote. Thank you for being open to trying new things, and for loving dogs as much as I do. You make my heart smile and every dog's tail wag.

There are a multitude of reasons to thank my family, but mainly for always supporting every out-there endeavor I take on. Bless my parents and my siblings for putting up with my love (obsession?) for animals since I was a very young child. No matter how unique my interests, my parents, my siblings, and my nieces and nephews (Gabriel! Anthony! Amanda!) are always cheering me on.

To Jorge, my husband, my best friend, my constant pillar. I can always count on you for unfailing support and encouragement. All of the thank-yous in every language in the world would still not be enough to tell you how grateful I am for you.

And last but not least, to the dogs who have helped me understand empathy and love deeper than humanly possible: Comet, Maya, Noah, Reyna. You're all the best boys and girls.

About the Author

VANESSA ESTRADA MARIN is the director at Frolic, a unique facility specializing in dog-centric programming for kids in New York City. Her combined experiences planning events and activities for children on the Upper East Side and pet matchmaking as an adoption center manager at North Shore Animal League America give her a unique perspective and the expertise to write this book. A lifelong animal lover and child at heart, Vanessa lives in Queens with her husband, Jorge, and their Chihuahua mix rescue, Reyna.

About frolic

FROLIC is a 1,500-square-foot space on the Upper East Side of Manhattan, where we take interactive and educational to a whole new level. Truly unique, Frolic is home to four friendly career change service dogs. Visitors come here to meet Patience, Chichy, Huxley, and Murray while simultaneously learning about man's best friend from Frolic's dog-loving experts. We support the community through various after-school programs, camps, specialized courses such as Overcoming Fear of Dogs and Canine Companion (how to have/care for a dog), and birthday parties. Frolic hosts special events held on-site and off-site. We have worked with Girl Scouts of America and organize school field trips.

Learn More:

WWW.FROLICKIDS.COM